Praise for *When Trouble Finds You*

"This is a *remarkable* account of persevering in a world filled with indescribable challenges. It incites each reader to confront the issues impacting our children on a daily basis. I never would have guessed life dealt Toni so many opportunities to give up. This book is a must-read for anyone serious about protecting children."

Steve Monaco
Retired corporate vice president
Motorola, Inc.

"Toni's story is absolutely amazing, and I am honored and blessed to know her. It is truly remarkable how she has managed to overcome such adversity and pain in her life walk. I have been supportive of abused and at-risk children for years, and I know they will certainly be inspired and encouraged by her story. Having read this, I am committed to following Toni's example and doing my part to help these children by inspiring them to overcome life's struggles and ensuing pain. No one, especially a child, should have to live through such torment and distress. Please accept this as a personal invitation to join Toni and change the lives of children because it shouldn't hurt to be a kid."

Tim Ashley
Vice president, operations
Cable industry

"We all have a story to tell, and Toni reveals how she overcame abandonment, sexual molestation, anger, and bitterness to become the strong wife, mother, and professional she is today."

Cynthia Dickens
US human resources sales lead
Biopharmaceuticals industry

"Societally, we have become desensitized to the realities of child abuse. Far too often, we shake our heads in dismay while providing a perfunctory comment about the travesties of the abuse and impact on the child. But have you ever looked into a child's eyes and understood that pain or the horror that was being carried inside? Toni's story allows us to look into *her* eyes and see this torment as we poignantly feel her loss of self, faith, and the desire to live. This is truly a story the world needs to hear!"

Dr. Christopher Anne Robinson-Easley
CEO, Enlightening Management Consultants, Inc.
Author of *Our Children – Our Responsibilities: Saving the Youth We Are Losing to Gangs*

"Extraordinary. A must-read book that speaks to the recovery of the human spirit. In these pages, Toni takes us on a journey through her personal experience—which could have broken most of us, minimized our core beliefs, and shifted our personal power. Instead, Toni shows each of us that no matter what history has presented, it *does not* have to define our future. This book invites each of us to consider the path from which we've come to create a better trail on which to move ahead. A book worth reading and sharing with anyone who is experiencing personal adversity."

Maureen O'Brien
CEO, MOF
O'Brien & Sons

"*When Trouble Finds You* creates awareness around crucial moments impacting the lives of abused children, their current and future relationships, and our world. I *promise* it will change the way you see the world and encourage you to build stronger relationships with children. They need us!"

Tyronne Stoudemire
Principal, diversity and inclusion
Mercer, Inc.

"An *inspiring* story of perseverance! Knowing Toni today, it is both difficult and enrapturing to read the story of her beginnings. I found myself reading the next chapter and the next and the next to find out when and how she finds the strength to transform from the little girl in this book to the Toni we know today. This book will stir you and provide a sharpened lens with which to view your own world of challenges."

Jill Blanchard
Senior marketing vice president, client services and business development
Consumer goods industry

"Fasten your seat belts to go on this emotional ride. Prepare for sudden jolts of the author's reality. When the book is over, you'll never forget her transformation or the young girls and women who need you to respond to this book as a call to action."

Candi Castleberry Singleton
Founder and chair
Dignity and Respect Campaign

"If you're interested in helping people who have been abused, this book will show you how to influence the behaviors of others. Carter reveals the deep thoughts of people who have been abused, shedding light on how to help them through their pain. This book is a must-read for everyone serious about helping families in need."

Rebecca Darr
Executive director
Women In Need Growing Stronger (WINGS)

"There is no one-size-fits-all solution for people experiencing challenges. However, this book reveals adaptable strategies for creating the life you want to live. Even if the odds are stacked against you, you'll find hope in these pages."

Dr. Thomas W. Nowaskey
Dentist

"This book is a call to action for people who have the courage to help protect innocent children. We must seek to understand the complexities of child abuse. Doing so will assist us in making the world a better place for all children. This story will change your life forever."

Jeanette Kilo-Smith
Vice president, human resources
World's largest employer

"A moving memoir. Toni Carter's story is one of continuing triumph over early tragedy. She shows us what it really means to make lemonade out of life's lemons. She refused to be a stigmatized statistic. She chose to be a purpose-driven victor rather than a passive and perpetual victim. Toni reminds us that we can all be conquerors in our own lives if we just believe in ourselves."

Rashaanda Cook
Vice president, organization development and chief learning officer
Large U.S. healthcare organization

"*When Trouble Finds You* is a life-changing must-read! This book taps into an issue that impacts our relationships, our lives, the lives of our children, and our world. It will transform your thoughts in ways you never imagined. If you can read only one book this year, let it be this one!"

Larissa Williams Staples
Corporate inclusive diversity manager
Largest P&C insurance company

"*Life changing!* This book is a testament to how one can overcome against all odds. The challenges in this book could have destroyed Toni, but the Lord has a great plan for her life. I see a strong, confident, and resilient woman. I knew Toni's story was an interesting one but never thought her struggles reached this magnitude. This book is much needed for our communities, because our children are being affected in all the ways she describes. Thank you, Toni, for sharing your life and being a spokeswoman for our children."

Evelyn Lewis Brown
Non-profit executive director
Author of *Bound and Unaware*

"*Courageous! When Trouble Finds You* is a powerful story and riveting reality, relating details often overlooked in life-altering events. It left me speechless! I've known Toni for twenty years, and as I read each page, I lived each moment of pain she endured. This is a moving reminder of a life that could have spiraled into the abyss of nothingness, but Toni overcame and is a phenomenal woman."

Joyace G. Ussin
Registered nurse and executive director
Clarion Call Women's Ministry

"Carter has exposed the tactics of abusers! This book will impact the way you think about influencing and protecting young people. It is a must-read that will increase your awareness and encourage you to help change the world."

Dr. Marty Martin
Director and associate professor
DePaul University

"Through her talent, Toni Carter has provided a heartfelt, honest reminiscence. She has provided insight into another life, a life that many might live or encounter briefly but which most refuse to acknowledge. Enduring the grief of rape, incest, impregnation, physical and mental abuse, and loneliness, Toni has used thought-provoking words to bring our attention to the mind-boggling heartbreak of life. Through her personal account of a life-not-worth-living, she has provided an opportunity for others to succeed far beyond the person they might believe resides within them. We might not be able to choose the lifestyle we inherit, but with God's compassion and wisdom, we can choose to overcome and grow. I am pleased to endorse Toni's work of art and commend her ability to share insight into another life with an intimacy that most of us would dare not reveal."

Lori J. Mitchell
Village clerk and friend

"Toni writes with clarity and power. *When Trouble Finds You* is an incredible story of overcoming the impossible, a testament that you can come from nowhere and still end up somewhere. If you believe it, you can most certainly achieve it. It's a great story."

Devin C. Hughes
Chief inspiration officer
Author of *Contrast: A Biracial Man's Journey to Desegregate His Past*

"My mother. My role model. My inspiration. With *When Trouble Finds You*, my mother is confronting her past, overcoming, and inspiring others to do the same. I am honored to be the child of a phenomenal woman."

Candes Carter
Student, Southern Illinois University Edwardsville
Master Public Administration, August 2013

When
Trouble
Finds YOU

Overcoming
Child Abuse, Teen Pregnancy, Domestic Violence,
and Discovering the Remarkable Power of the Human Spirit

Toni L. Coleman Carter

Writers of the Round Table Press
PO Box 511, Highland Park, IL 60035

www.roundtablecompanies.com

Publisher: Corey Michael Blake
Executive Editor: Katie Gutierrez
Editor: Nadja Baer
Discussion Guide and Lessons Learned Editor: Ivan Alexander
Post Production: David Charles Cohen
Directoress of Happiness: Erin Cohen
Director of Author Services: Kristin Westberg
Facts Keeper: Mike Winicour
Front Cover Concept: William Lee
Back Cover: Analee Paz
Interior Design and Layout: Sunny DiMartino
Proofreading: Rita Hess
Last Looks: Sunny DiMartino
Digital Book Conversion: Sunny DiMartino
Digital Publishing: Sunny DiMartino

Printed in the United States of America
First Edition: April 2013

Author's Note
This book is based on my life story. Conversations have been reconstructed to the
best of my recollection, for learning and teaching purposes only.

Library of Congress Cataloging-in-Publication Data
Carter, Toni L. Coleman
When trouble finds you: overcoming child abuse, teen pregnancy, domestic
violence, and discovering the remarkable power of the human spirit /
Toni L. Coleman Carter.—1st ed. p. cm.
ISBN Paperback 978-1-939418-04-3   ISBN Digital 978-1-939418-10-4
Library of Congress Control Number: 2013937365

RTC Publishing is an imprint of Writers of the Round Table, Inc.
Writers of the Round Table Press and the RTC Publishing logo
are trademarks of Writers of the Round Table, Inc.

Contents

Part 1
When Everything Goes Wrong!

Part 2
Activating the Power Within

Part 3
Knowledge: The Key to Unlocking Destiny

Part 4
Resources for Self-Empowerment

This book is dedicated to increasing awareness around issues impacting our children, while inspiring the human spirit!

Foreword

Before you start reading *When Trouble Finds You*, know this: it is a harrowing journey. From Toni Carter's childhood sexual abuse to her teen pregnancy, to the challenges and eventual triumphs of her adult life and career, Toni sugarcoats nothing . . . even when you might want her to.

Yet, even through the difficulty of her journey, Toni offers hope.

I had the pleasure of meeting this vibrant lady in 2000 when she was a student in one of my undergraduate classes. Shortly afterward, she became one of my graduate students. We stayed connected over the years, and as I watched her grow and mature, I marveled at her determination, faith, and focus. Her motivation and energy, combined with a disarming groundedness, were refreshing both inside and outside the classroom. Toni has many astounding characteristics. Until I read her book, though, I never suspected all she went through as a child and teenager. Now I know her on another level. I know her to be a fighter.

Toni's story allows you to see from her eyes the inner turmoil an abused child faces. She lets us in to her darkest moments—her loss of self, faith, and desire to live—and then, through a deep determination to rise above, she demonstrates the possibility of not letting such tragedies define us.

Toni's success as an adult, however, should not lull the

reader to passivity. Too many children do not overcome the trauma of child abuse; whether it is verbal, sexual, physical, psychological, or any combination, abuse leaves behind life-long scars. While some abused children grow up learning to hide their pain and resist emotional connection, others grow up acting out their suffering in disruptive ways. The original trauma thus lives on.

In our society, we have become desensitized to the realities of child abuse—one of Toni's key messages. Far too often, we shake our heads in dismay, offering a perfunctory comment about the travesties of the abuse and impact to the child. But have you ever looked into a child's eyes and understood that pain—or the horror being carried inside? Toni lets us—indeed, compels us—to do just that. In so doing, she helps us understand the critical roles we play in saving the life of a child. We cannot walk away.

This story is Toni's legacy to society. It is her reminder and call to action: if we suspect someone of abusing children, we have a responsibility to take action.

I am blessed to know Mrs. Toni Carter, to be asked to write the foreword to her book, to share a part of her life, and to see her tell a story that takes so much courage to share. Children are our future. Each one is a gift and far too precious to lose. As parents, caregivers, educators, relatives, friends, and even strangers, it is our responsibility to help them grow into happy, healthy, productive adults. That is the only hope for betterment of this world.

Thank you, Toni, for having the courage and faith to step out and tell your story. It is one the world deeply needs to hear!

—Dr. Christopher Anne Robinson-Easley

Author of *Our Children, Our Responsibilities: Saving the Youth We Are Losing to Gangs*

CEO, Enlightening Management Consultants, Inc.

www.enlighteningmanagementconsultants.com

Introduction

On a fall afternoon, I walked across the hall from my bedroom to the bathroom. There, I rifled through our mirrored medicine cabinet, bypassing typical over-the-counter items in favor of the first bottle of painkillers I found. With my fingers wrapped around the slim cylinder, I returned to my room and closed the door. As the sun gilded the edges of my window curtains, I emptied the whole bottle of pills into my hand. I stared at them for a long time before filling my mouth and chasing them down with water. Then I sank into bed and closed my eyes.

As I waited to die, I wasn't thinking about losing my father or my faith. I wasn't thinking about my mother, her heavy hands and long absences, which often left me in charge of my four younger siblings. I wasn't thinking of the many people who had inappropriately touched me, and my thoughts didn't land on my boyfriend, who was too busy pursuing other girls to notice the pain in my eyes. I never thought about the person who would find me lying in bed with an empty bottle of pills on the floor. I wasn't even thinking of my unborn baby, though my belly was stretched far and thin with her eight-month growth. All I could think about was escaping my pain.

I was fifteen.

One of my younger brothers found me. At first, he thought I was taking a nap. But soon my mother was shaking me, holding the pill bottle and demanding to know if I had emp-tied it inside me. Groggily, I said yes. My mother rushed me to the hospital, and when I woke up after having my stomach pumped, all I could think was, *Why am I still here?* Exhaustion pressed me into my bed, and I couldn't help but wonder: how much more would I have to endure? Why couldn't they just let me die?

When you are young and pregnant in a small southern town—or anywhere, really—many people want to punish you. My mom chose to drag me to and from the Adams County Health Department for appointments instead of taking me around the corner to see Dr. Sherman, the family obstetrician/gynecologist. This process always took half a day, because she made us walk the six miles each way. My friends' parents, meanwhile, prohibited their children from spending time with me because I was a "bad influence." As my belly grew, so did my hopelessness, isolation, shame, and depression.

My misery blinded me to people who cared about me, even though they stared me right in the face. Hidden in my darkness were my Grandma Liza, my aunts Sarah and Joyce, my Uncle Joe, and my cousins LindaKay, Nina, and Chanell. Any one of them would have picked up the phone if I'd bothered to call.

After I had first my daughter, Candes, and then my son, John, things slowly began to change. However, things got harder before they got better, and until recently, I was never able to talk about my suicide attempt. I was too embarrassed. Only now, looking back, can I tell others in similar situations it's never as bad as it looks—and people care more than you know. We all have at least one person who truly cares about us.

Trouble has found me on many occasions, and life has

dealt me extraordinary challenges. Because of those challenges, I have a special place in my heart for people who are hurting. It doesn't matter if it's from abuse, rejection, loss of a loved one, sickness, or something that makes them feel worthless—trust me, I know and I understand. If you know people who cannot see through their pain, please give them a copy of this book. It's proof the two of us care: I wrote it just for them, and you cared enough to give it to them. Together, we can help change their world.

And if you're struggling with adversity yourself, know this: *despite what has happened to you, you can make it; it's never too late to create the life you want!*

OVERCOMER

Part 1

When Everything Goes Wrong!

Chapter 1

Life and Its Surprises

The New Orleans sun beat down on our bare arms and legs as my siblings and I vied for our dad's attention. The afternoon was muggy, the air thick, as we played in the parking lot outside our apartment. Dad wasn't allowed inside; he and Mama weren't on speaking terms. But during the infrequent times he was around, it was as if he never wanted to be anywhere else. He looked at me with clear, direct brown eyes that assured me I had his undivided attention; *I* was his girl! It made saying goodbye so much harder.

"I've got to get going, baby," he said, glancing down at his watch.

"But you just got here!" I protested. The sunlight tinted Dad's neatly trimmed Afro and bounced off his smooth, clean-shaven face. He was handsome.

"What should I bring you for your birthday?" he asked.

I was turning seven in a few weeks and didn't even have to think about my answer. "A bike!" With a bicycle, I'd be free to go wherever I wanted—though where I thought I'd go at that age is a mystery to me!

He gave me a smile that looked like my own. "Then that's what I'll bring you."

I was so excited about the prospect of my own bike I don't remember him leaving that day. The next few weeks crawled by in anticipation. I was watching TV in the living room with my siblings the day a phone call changed our lives. Mama got up and walked to the kitchen. At first, I didn't pay attention to what she was saying—I was daydreaming about my new bike. Dad would buy it for me. I knew he would.

Then: "*What?*" Mama almost yelled.

My dream started to fade. Something was wrong.

"No—that's impossible . . ." Mama turned her back to us as she listened. Her head with its short, dark hair shook slowly back and forth. "How did this happen?" Another minute passed, and her back straightened. ". . . All right. All right." She cleared her throat, her tone moving from emotional to logical. "Let me make some calls."

It could have been a thousand other things, but immediately it hit me: I no longer had a dad.

· · ·

In my mind, I'm a small-town girl. The truth, though, is Natchez, Mississippi is bigger than the way my memory recalls it. It's a city with Native American roots, founded by the Natchez tribe, which later became home to the Cherokees, Chickasaws, Choctaws, and Creeks; although they were pushed out by French armed forces in the 1700s. It's a city whose big box stores like Walmart, JCPenney, and Sears draw people from surrounding towns within an hour's drive. When I grew up in Natchez, it was a city of invisible borders. There was a white side and a black side, and the two sides, because of racial sensibilities, rarely met.

Like nearly everyone from the original city, my family is

part Indian. My maternal grandmother, Eliza, grew up there and had her first child, Michael, when she was eighteen years old. Seven years later, my mother, Sheila, was born. After my grandmother divorced her husband, she realized picking cotton didn't bring in enough income to provide for two children. So, leaving them behind with her mother, Madea, she moved to New Orleans at her cousin Ellen's urging. She eventually took a job behind Ellen's bar, while attending school to become a dietitian. What little she made, she sent back to Sheila and Michael. Nevertheless, her checks meant nothing to Mama; she felt abandoned long after her mother returned to get her, complete with a job in the Orleans Parish school system.

My dad, Robert Coleman, Sr., came to Natchez from D'Lo, a "one-mile" town two hours away, on a football scholarship to Natchez College. He was a star player with a promising future and an interest in becoming a Baptist preacher. Mama was an eighteen-year-old high school senior. I don't know how they met or fell in love, what drew them to each other or eventually tore them apart. All I know is Mama became pregnant with me while they were just dating. I was born Toni LaVell Peters, and after they were married, someone altered the writing on my birth certificate to read Toni LaVell Coleman. The rest of my parents' love story will always be a mystery—at least to me.

Since my parents couldn't raise a family in my father's dorm room, I stayed with Aunt Sarah—my grandmother's younger sister—and Uncle Albert Hughes for the first few years of my life. Mama checked in from time to time, but she was hardly out of her teens yet; her interest was in having fun, not changing diapers and losing hours of sleep for midnight feedings. The Hugheses became my primary caregivers. They fed me, clothed me, and raced to the convenience store in the middle of the night for milk when I wouldn't stop crying. However, they couldn't raise me forever. They had five children of their own, so I was sent to live with my maternal grandparents.

My grandparents met in their mid-forties and had both been married before. Granddad—we called him Jesse because he didn't think he was old enough to be anybody's granddaddy—had five boys with his first wife, and Grandma had Michael and my mother, but all seven were out of the house before I was born. Five or six years into their relationship, Grandma consulted with her priest about marrying Jesse. He questioned her decision.

"Why do you want to marry him?" her priest asked. "Over the years, you've seen for yourself how he likes to drink and carouse. That lifestyle doesn't seem like a good match for your personality."

Grandma listened and nodded quietly. "I hear what you're saying," she told him. Then she married Jesse anyway—a decision she only regretted aloud when she was upset.

Jesse was as loud and lively as Grandma was quiet and reserved; you could walk into a room and never notice she was there, but Jesse's presence lingered in the air hours after he departed. He was a straight shooter and never had a problem letting anyone know what was on his mind, while Grandma swallowed every negative emotion with pride. Even when he got himself a girlfriend in their own neighborhood, buying her new appliances and anything else she needed, my grandmother said nothing. Years later, her strongest reproach was, "Remember the time you mistreated me with that little woman down the street?" Quiet compliance was ingrained in her nature. She let people take advantage of her, never losing her temper the way Mama—and eventually I—would do.

For me, a toddler by the time I moved in with them, my grandparents' home was a comfortable, quiet haven. Immaculately clean and scented with mothballs, it filled me with a sense of safety. I don't remember missing Mama or even being aware there *was* something to miss. At two, I was already adaptable.

My first sister was born in 1972, just a few months before Dad graduated from college. By then, he'd left his bright football future behind and joined the U.S. Army to support his family. Mama lived with him for a while on base; the two of them shared a small home with my little sister. By the time I was three, my mother was pregnant with twin boys, rounding out the family with four children.

One evening, Grandma opened the door to find my parents standing outside with a uniformed police officer.

"That's her," Mama said accusingly. She was aggressive and used to bullying my grandmother into getting her way. She leveled Grandma with a scathing accusation. "We've been asking her to give Toni back, but she won't."

Grandma stood there in shock—my parents hadn't warned her they were coming or even hinted they wanted me back. My dad kept his eyes on the ground while Mama called her own mother a kidnapper. I'd been living with Grandma and Jesse for two years, but I later learned no paperwork had ever changed hands. Jesse wasn't home, so my grandmother was at a loss. After a few moments of stunned silence, she opened the door a bit wider. "Well," she said sadly, "come in."

Later in life, I'd come to resent her habitual compliance, but at the time I didn't understand what was happening. I left with my parents that day, not a thing explained and not a bag packed, and Grandma turned to food as her comfort.

Dad called her back later to explain. "I had nothing to do with that," he said into the phone, keeping his voice low so Mama couldn't hear. "It was all her idea."

"If you say so," Grandma said. She didn't believe him, but she wouldn't refuse his attempt at an apology.

We lived on a military base for a while after that, but Dad was in and out of Mississippi as his orders dictated. He was around so infrequently I have no memories of him during their marriage. Not long after they reclaimed me, Mama and Daddy joined the long-standing family tradition of divorce.

Mama—young, reckless, and looking for love in all the wrong places—didn't stay single for long. She remarried quickly, and my youngest sister was born in 1975. Fortunately, we all loved Bob, our stepdad. Like my grandmother, he was gentle and soft-spoken. He avoided confrontation and strove for peace. Even after Mama had his daughter, he cared for the four of us as if we were his own. Bob made sure we had supper on the table when Mama ran the streets. But still, he wasn't my dad.

Things were going as well as could be expected when one day, out of the blue, my mother decided she hated our small town life.

"Let's go," she said, clapping her hands together in the doorway of my room. "Everyone start packing. We're leaving by the end of the week."

That was the extent of the discussion. I was five and used to sudden moves by now. Mama wasn't the type to have conversations with kids; she believed kids should stay in their place. She issued commands and we followed them. That was how, quite suddenly, all seven of us ended up in one of the worst neighborhoods in New Orleans.

We moved into an isolated housing development called the Fischer Projects. The Fischer was built adjacent to the Mississippi River Bridge. The bridge, the Donner Canal, and a Southern Pacific Railroad line separated the community from the rest of the city. The fourteen low-slung buildings, interspersed with parkland, were like their own city, with the residents governing themselves—often by violence.

Less than a year after we moved in, my mother accused a neighbor's kid of running over my younger sister, Erica, on her bike.

"What do you think you're doing?" Mama yelled at the kid. She pressed a crying Erica close to her while she yelled. "Didn't your mother teach you how to ride a bike? You could have killed her!"

The kid glared back at my mother before hopping back on the bike and pedaling away. Mama took Erica back home, but it wasn't long before she heard from the kid's mother. This woman was not about to let Mama disrespect her or verbally abuse her kid. She showed up at our apartment foaming at the mouth.

Bob gave Mama a worried look. "You're going to have to leave now," he said softly to the other mother, edging her out the door and locking it as Mama rushed to close all the windows. The cheap plastic blinds rustled as they dropped and banged against the window frames.

The woman pounded on the door. "Why are you hiding from me? Come tell me all that stuff you said to my daughter. I dare you. I swear, if you ever say anything to my child again, I will—"

"Get in your room," Mama told us. "All of you."

We didn't move quickly enough. Mama grabbed my arm and pushed me into the bedroom behind my siblings. The door locked with an audible click. In the small room we shared, Erica, our twin brothers Tracy and Stacy, and little sister LaDonna huddled together. We were little, far too young to understand what was happening, but we understood the urgency in Mama's voice. Bob's soothing tone drifted through the tense air of the apartment, but Mama wasn't listening to him.

The other woman kept pounding on the door and screaming, "If you ever say one word to my child again, I will kill you! Do you hear me?"

Mama matched her pitch and volume. Their voices rose and tangled until I couldn't tell who was doing the cursing. The apartment was so small, the walls so thin, it felt to me as if the whole world were shaking. In my head, if the woman broke through the door, there was no telling what would happen.

"I'm calling Jesse," I heard Bob say. A minute later, he said, "You've got to get over here. Sheila is into it with a neighbor, and the situation is out of hand."

In the Fischer Projects, if you called the police, they might stop by if someone had been shot. Maybe. Calling Jesse was a much safer bet—especially since, like a true country man, he never left home without his gun. He knew he had to be serious with "city folks." He raced over right away, and soon gunshots filled the air. My siblings and I clung to each other.

"Are we going to die?" Erica whispered, crying.

"Of course we're not going to die!" I hissed back, but my heart was pounding in my throat.

Jesse held off the other family while Mama rushed into the bedroom, grabbing baby LaDonna and gesturing the rest of us off the floor.

"Come on," she said. "Hurry, we're leaving."

I hesitated. I was as scared as my siblings were, but the bedroom seemed safer than the craziness outside.

"Move it!" Mama yelled. "Come on, Jesse's waiting. Let's go."

We left with the clothes on our backs and nothing more. Years later, Jesse would laugh about that day, reminding us how he'd "cleaned house," but at the time, we were scared stiff and pressed tightly against one another as he roared away from the Fischer Projects.

After that, the seven of us, displaced and confused, moved into my grandparents' house. They had purchased the West Bank home the year I was born. Previously, they'd lived in half of a duplex they had purchased on the East Bank many years before, collecting enough rent from it to pay the bank note on their new property. Despite their modest incomes and underprivileged upbringings, they made some wise investment decisions that allowed them to accommodate us in their home until a slot in another housing project became available. It was called the Desire, of all things.

The Desire Project was built on a swampland—previously a landfill—in the Upper Ninth Ward. Like the Fischer Projects, the Desire was segregated from the rest of the city by several canals and railroad tracks on all four sides. It was a place where bad things happened to good people—even children.

My school was only a mile away from the new apartment, but I had to be on constant alert when I walked there. Fights broke out in the courtyard, and either Mama or Bob was always with us when we went outside to play. I felt the seedy undercurrent—a hurried exchange, raised voices, half-dressed men and women wandering—but was too young to articulate what made me anxious. Looking back, I can't imagine what my mother was thinking, moving there with small children.

Dad visited from time to time, but the image of him I will forever see in my memory is when he knocked on the door a few weeks before my seventh birthday. He didn't come into the apartment; he had also remarried, and Mama wouldn't let my stepmom into her home, nor was she on speaking terms with Dad. I stood outside with my sister and the twins to visit with him. That was the day he promised to buy me a bike for my birthday. It was the last time I saw him.

My mother didn't sit us down to tell us what happened, but I pieced together the facts from her telephone conversations. Dad had gone to his local VA hospital to have his tonsils removed. They gave him the wrong anesthesia, and after his eyes closed, they never opened again. Instead of a bike for my birthday, I got a funeral.

The wake lasted for hours, and we sat there the whole time, stuck in a room with a dead body. Mama filled a roll of film with pictures of Dad's wake, including several shots of his body. She wanted to make a scrapbook. What could anyone want with a book full of death? As soon as it was over, we were shuffled off to my paternal grandparents' house and put to bed. I couldn't sleep. The room was dark, and everywhere I looked, ghosts leaped out of my imagination. Faces took shape on the walls. Hands reached toward me. I clenched my eyes shut and burrowed deeply under the covers, but I couldn't hide from Daddy's face. My heart was full of pain.

The next morning, the sun was barely illuminating the leaves on trees when we woke up for the funeral. No one even mentioned the fact that it was my birthday. At the service, I sat staring at the back of two grown-ups' heads. I couldn't even see what was going on at my father's casket. Angry, illogical thoughts filled my mind. *Who are these people and why are they sitting in the front row? Robert Lee Coleman, Sr. is my dad! I should be sitting there. He said he was coming back, and he's not here.* I was mad at my dad for not bringing me the bike like he had promised, sad because he was never coming back, and scared by all of the emotions I couldn't seem to process on my own.

Dad was the baby of a family of six, and his brothers and sisters each had several children. It seemed as if a hundred people were crowded in my grandparents' house after the service for the repast. While my mom argued with Dad's second wife over who would take home the American flag draped on his coffin, my Grandma Mary came to console me with a tomato sandwich.

"Here, honey," she said. "It's from the garden."

She watched until I bit into the sandwich but soon left to see about Grandpa Joe. He was taking his youngest son's death the hardest and would grieve himself to death only one month later. In the meantime, six children—the four of us and the two kids my dad had with his second wife—had lost their father, and no one stopped to ask how we felt or if we needed anything. I'd never felt more alone in such a crowded place—or more uncertain as to what would happen next.

Chapter 2

Be Careful
Who You Trust

After my father's funeral, our family settled into our new normal. I nursed a quiet anger at Dad for abandoning me and withdrew into myself. I was like a snail—a small soft shape covered by a protective shell but far from unbreakable.

Mom, who managed a McDonald's restaurant, and Bob, a general contractor, both worked long hours and occasional Saturdays to support the family. Mama asked her friend Ms. Carrie, who lived just downstairs in the same apartment building, for help with us. Ms. Carrie was a nice woman, stout with short hair and honey-colored skin. She was also a working mom, and I overheard her telling Mama she had problems controlling her kids. She had six or seven children, but the three youngest—Penny, Pam, and Andre—still lived at home. Andre was the oldest at around sixteen, Penny was a year or so younger, and Pam was the youngest at twelve. In what seemed to be a win-win—Ms. Carrie would know where her kids were, and Mama would get some help babysitting—Mama asked whichever one of them was available to watch us when she and Bob were out. The kids were nice and polite in front of adults, but things changed the moment the apartment door closed.

"Have a nice day at work," Pam called out after my mother's retreating form in the hallway. Mama gave a half-hearted wave over her shoulder. She didn't even look back.

My siblings and I watched from the corners of our eyes. My heart instinctively sped up. We were animals of prey, feeling the trap closing in on us. Who would it be today? The door closed with a quiet *click*. Bile rose in my stomach.

"You," Pam said, pointing to me. "Get in the closet."

My brothers and sisters scurried out of the living room; no doubt they were relieved that today I was the chosen one. I shuffled to the front hall closet and sat down in the dark amongst the musty smell of coats and shoes. Pam's shadow loomed over me, her body blocking the light from the living room. She scowled down at me. "You tell anybody what happens here, I'll beat you."

I knew it was true. All of us had been punched or slapped for resisting our babysitters' demands at one time or another, and it never changed the result. Now we just obeyed.

Pam slipped into the closet and closed the door behind her, plunging us both into darkness. Her elbow bumped against my shoulder, and the faint rustle of fabric said she was taking off her shirt. She grabbed my hand and put my palm against her breast. Her skin was warm. She leaned back against the wall as I fondled her breasts. My stomach churned with discomfort.

Even though I didn't understand sexual acts or why she wanted me to touch her, I sensed what she was making me do wasn't right. The sense of wrongness—the confusing strangeness of it all—was choking. As my eyes adjusted to the darkness, Pam took my fingers and moved them toward the waistband of her pants. *I don't want to do this!* I wanted to shout. I wanted to run out of the closet and out the front door and never come back. But then who would watch out for my younger siblings? Certainly not Mama.

When she was finished with me, Pam pulled her shirt back over her head. "You tell anybody and I'll beat you. I'm not playing with you. Do you understand me?" She blocked the door, her hand around the knob.

"I get it," I said quietly, though not without a touch of defiance. I looked at the ground, which I could still barely make out in the darkness, until Pam opened the door and walked out. Now that she was done with me, she was off to make sure the other kids hadn't dirtied the house. Mama, like Grandma, kept an immaculate home. You could eat off our floors, and if you couldn't, you'd *feel* Mama's displeasure.

When Pam was out of sight, I ran out of the closet and into to my room. My sisters looked up when the door opened, their eyes round and frightened, but they relaxed when they saw me. I threw myself onto my bed and closed my eyes. Anger festered in my belly, making me curl my hands into fists. Why did Dad have to die? Why did Mama have to leave us with Ms. Carrie's children? Why did they want to hurt us? I couldn't make myself believe this was how life was supposed to be, but I didn't have any other version to compare it to. All I could do was get through it.

Going through this sort of abuse at home, by people my family trusted, caused my siblings and me to become very distrustful of others. Part of me was always keenly aware of my surroundings. Whether I was in a classroom, on a bus, or at a playground, I was never fully engaged or lost in the moment. I was too busy watching everyone else's movements. I never knew what they might do.

In school, I started getting into trouble for acting out. When I was in second grade, my teachers started warning each other, "This girl is bad. You need to watch her." Back then, in Catholic school, they were allowed to whip you as punishment for *badness.* My teachers slapped my open palm with a ruler for minor infractions, while the principal took a paddle to me for larger offenses.

One day, I said a bad word during class. My teacher came over to my desk, wrapped one hand around my arm, and pulled me to my feet. She marched me to the principal's office, where she made me confess my sin. The principal called my mother, and my punishment became a spectacle.

The principal led a small troop of adults and me to the girls' bathroom. She pushed me in front of one of the sinks. In the mirror, I could see my teacher, my mother, and the principal all staring at me. Mama stood with her arms crossed over her chest, her lips pursed in anger. Inside, I glared back at all of them, but my reflection in the mirror remained calm and impassive. The situation was ridiculous—I learned bad language from listening to adults, but here they were, punishing me for using it. The principal grabbed a bar of soap from the sink and made me wash my own mouth out with it. The soap tasted bitter, making me gag over the sink. When I returned to class, my eyes were red-rimmed and raw from trying not to cry.

Even though I acted out, I made sure my grades didn't suffer. One bad grade was enough to incur Mama's wrath—you'd get home and think your life was over. I'm not sure she knew why, but bad grades were a punishable offense. Anything she held in her hand—a belt, an extension cord—was liable to make painful contact with skin.

At home, I found other ways to push my boundaries. After Mama hit me, I wanted to unnerve her. She kept an old black rotary phone in the living room as decoration. One afternoon, I picked up the receiver and called heaven. I spoke loudly, knowing my mother could hear everything I said.

"Hi, can I speak to my dad?" I waited as though there were someone on the other end of the line. "Hi, Dad."

"Ain't nobody on that phone," Mama said from the kitchen. "That phone doesn't even work."

I kept talking, pretending I hadn't heard her.

She walked into my range of vision. "Hang that phone up." *Or else,* the edge on her voice added silently.

Adrenaline made my heart beat faster as I tested my limits. I eyeballed her, the phone pressed to the side of my face. "Mama's been beating on me again." Again, I paused for a response, listening to heavy silence. "Yeah, and the other day she took off for hours and just left us here by ourselves."

"Toni Coleman, you hang up that phone before I hit you upside the head with it!"

No one was talking back to me, but it didn't matter. I was getting a reaction from her and I liked it. There is an element of accountability to hearing your child state aloud the things you've done, and Mama didn't want to hear the way I perceived the things that were happening to me. That was too bad. Due to the strain between Mama and Grandma, I didn't have any adults I could talk to about the abuse—which was doubly sad, because at the time Grandma was only thirty minutes away on the other side of the bridge. I considered talking to Bob, but I didn't think he would believe me. Even if he did, he'd just tell Mama, and then I'd be in more trouble. I was trapped in a terrifying downward spiral, and these imaginary phone calls were my only chance to express my pain. Plus, even if no one was listening, making Mama uncomfortable was a small victory in my troubled world.

We lived in the projects until I was about ten years old. That year, we received a settlement check from the VA hospital in Jackson where Dad died. I don't know how much was in that check—I had no concept of money and no idea why we got it—but I knew it was a lot. That check became the new point of contention between Grandma and Mama.

Grandma knew Mama wasn't responsible and would either waste or spend all of the money on herself. So she immediately enlisted the help of an attorney and went to court in Natchez. She wanted to make sure the money was put into a trust until all of us children turned twenty-one. Mama found her own lawyer and a battle ensued. They fought about it on the phone constantly.

"Why should I listen to anything you have to say?" Mama shouted into the receiver while we sat at the dinner table. "You left me, went to New Orleans, and never came back!"

Grandma's voice crackled faintly across the line. "That money belongs to those kids. They're not going to have anything left when they grow up."

"You have no right to tell me what to do!"

"Your kids are going to need that money to go to school or buy a house someday, Diane," Grandma said, using her inexplicable nickname for my mother. "Listen to your mama."

"Madea is my mama, *Lil Liza*," Mama said, referring to her grandmother. "You leave me the hell alone." The phone slammed down in its cradle. I didn't dare look her in the eye.

In the end, my grandmother won, but not before Mama used some of the settlement to buy us a house just down the street from my Aunt Sarah in Vidalia. We left the projects and moved into a new house in a complex called The Park. Bob didn't make the move with us. I never knew why he and my mother divorced or even when they separated; I had enough of my own troubles to worry about to notice any deterioration in their relationship. Mary, another one of my aunts, lived directly across the street from us, so we had plenty of cousins within walking distance. The Park was home to many families with children. In my mind, life was good. We'd left Penny, Pam, and Andre and their yearlong abuse behind.

I never thought things could get worse than the Desire.

Chapter 3

Things Are Not Always What They Seem

Our new house had three bedrooms, two bathrooms, a living room, a kitchen, a dining area, and a long hallway that connected all of them. The sofa faced an open floor area we used as a living room. From there, I could see through the dining room and into the kitchen. Moving boxes cluttered the floor. Behind the house, more than half an acre of open, unfenced grass melded with the yards of our neighbors.

Mama pushed past me; the box in her arms knocked into my shoulder and threw me off balance.

"Go to your room and put your stuff away," she ordered. "We have a party to get ready for this weekend."

I obeyed. Mama ran the ship—if we had opinions, she expected us to keep them to ourselves.

The bedroom I shared with my sisters faced the front yard. Just outside our window, a light pole stood watch over the street. Mama had to pay extra for that light. Since the community was a fairly new development, proper street lighting hadn't been installed yet. A boy about my age played in the yard next door. He saw me looking at him and waved.

I stepped back from the window and retreated to where he couldn't see me.

Mama and a couple of her friends had planned a big backyard party to celebrate the purchase of her first house. It was the weekend we moved in, and all of my siblings were sent to someone else's house to get them out of Mama's hair. My reputation as a bad kid always preceded me, so none of her friends would take me in for the day. My Aunt Sarah and her kids must have been busy, or I am sure I would have been sent to their house. I was always welcomed there.

"Go sit in the living room and behave yourself," Mama said, steering me toward the sofa. Every cushion was in its place, and there wasn't so much as a stray sock on the floor. "Watch your cartoons. I don't want a bunch of playing and jumping around and all that crap, you hear me?"

I looked at the ground and nodded as she pointed for me to leave the kitchen.

While I flipped channels, the energy ramped up in the rest of the house. Laughter and gossip drifted out of the kitchen as Mama and her friends made pimento cheese dip and deviled eggs.

"Did you hear Lil Leo just got back this week?" I heard Mama ask during a commercial break.

"What does Big Leo think about that?"

"He's proud as can be of his boy, serving his country in the Marines."

That afternoon, a big silver keg arrived. Condensation dripped and sparkled in the hot sun as the deliveryman carted it around to the back of the house under Mama's direction.

Despite the excitement in the air, I couldn't participate in the party. It didn't start until after my eight o'clock bedtime, so I was in my room well before the festivities got going. Even with the air conditioner on, nights hit eighty degrees. I lay under a thin sheet as music played and people laughed and shouted. The murmur of good times lulled me to sleep.

I was startled awake by a warm hand on my waist.

"What's going on?" I tried to ask, rubbing the sleep out of my eyes.

"Shh," a voice hissed in the dimness. The hand stayed where it was.

A yawn rolled up from deep in my lungs. As I blinked, the room came into sharper focus. The light pole in the front yard threw a low light through the curtains, illuminating the empty beds where my sisters usually slept.

"Who—"

"Be quiet," the tall shadow at my side snapped. The mattress shifted underneath me as he rolled me onto my back.

I stared up through the haze of sleep, right at my cousin Lil Leo; the military crew cut told me this was the big hero the family was so proud of for serving his country. His eyes glinted in the low light, the only bright spots in his otherwise dark face. He smelled like sweat.

"Be quiet," he repeated as he glanced toward the bedroom door.

I followed his gaze. The master bathroom was only twenty feet away on the other side, but the bedroom door was closed. A lump of anxiety swelled in my throat.

Leo brought his face close to mine. "If you tell anybody what happens here, I will kill you and your family."

The anxious feeling solidified into a cold ball of fear. With Pam, Penny, and Andre, I'd known what to expect; I saw them coming in the daylight, and there were always other targets around. As heinous as it was, it was a shared experience. Here, in my bedroom, it was just Lil Leo and me. He was family, and an adult. What did he want with me?

"Don't make any noises." He pushed the sheet aside and slid his rough, man-sized hands up my legs.

My groggy mind struggled to make sense of what was happening. Being woken from my sleep like this—in my *bed*, my safe haven—was worse than anything I could have imagined. I felt defenseless, so caught off guard I couldn't even disengage my mind the way I had in the hall closet back in the Desire. I was *living* through every moment as Lil Leo pulled off my underpants and put a hand between my legs. His breathing quickened as his fingers worked.

The din of the party continued outside. I wanted to scream, to lash out, but his words rang in my head: *I'll kill you and your family.* I believed him and the crazy light in his eyes. It seemed like eternity as I lay there, too scared to move or make a sound while his fingers explored my body. Every so often, he glanced over his shoulder at the door, but his hands didn't stop. Sweat beaded on his forehead, sliding down the sides of his face before dripping from his chin onto my bed.

After he was satisfied, he just got up and left. The quiet click of the door shutting seemed to echo in my room. I lay still, afraid he hadn't really gone. *Did this really happen? But he's my cousin . . . why would he do that?*

The party went on, the guests—and Mama—oblivious to what had happened in my bedroom. Every time someone walked down the hall to use the bathroom, I froze, waiting to see if the footsteps were coming to my door. Fear and confusion kept me awake all night while the commotion of the party went into the wee hours of the morning.

The next day passed in a fog. I searched the entire house, trying to make sure Lil Leo wasn't hiding in a corner somewhere. Convinced he would kill us if I even *hinted* at what happened, I never said a word. The experience was left to curdle inside me, with no escape. After all, my only safe place, my bed, had been violated. At ten years old, I withdrew into a world of anger and confusion. I lost all interest in dolls and games; I don't remember being excited about anything after that. I was hopeless.

My inability to express what I was feeling manifested itself in physical outbursts. The boy who lived next door, Al, sat behind me in school. He seemed to like me, and he sometimes whispered to me during class. I hadn't minded so much before, but now things were different between me and everyone else in the world. Boys my age were prone to silliness, and I had no tolerance left for nonsense.

One afternoon, he tapped me on the shoulder. "I see you're wearing those pies again," he quietly taunted. He meant the beat-up Converse All-Stars I wore every day. "Toni and her no-name clothes." His breath tickled my ear.

My shoulder jerked involuntarily, trying to push away his words. The yellow number two pencil in my hand curved slightly in my tight grip. I could hear him laughing quietly behind me. The anger I'd been swallowing for weeks erupted.

I whipped around in my seat and glared at Al. With no warning, I drove the point of my pencil down into his hand. His skin resisted, but the sharp point of the graphite bit through it and sank down between the bones of his fingers.

Al let out a curdling scream, and pandemonium broke out in the classroom.

"Toni Coleman!" my teacher shouted as she raced to our side of the room.

Al shoved himself back from his desk, almost tipping it over. Pain and fury sparked in his eyes. I stood up and balled my hands into fists as I stared up into his face. He towered over me and outweighed me by at least sixty pounds, but I wasn't going to back down from the challenge.

My teacher stepped between us before things escalated into a fistfight. "What is going on back here?" She recoiled slightly when she saw Al's bleeding hand.

"She's crazy," Al said, holding his injury out as proof. Blood ran down past his wrist.

She prodded the back of his hand softly. "That's it. You're both going to principal's office right now."

Al glared daggers at me over her head.

The principal didn't say anything to me directly. Both of our parents were called in—Mama because I was suspended, who knew for how long, and Al's because they thought he might need an updated tetanus shot. His parents picked him up long before Mama arrived.

She was already livid when she came to take me home, and things didn't improve when she talked to the principal.

"Al's parents have inquired about the cost of his hospital visit," he told her.

"And?" Mama stood with her arms crossed, impatient to get out of the office.

"I'm afraid the school isn't liable for your daughter's actions. I am sure they will be in contact with you as soon as they get him home from the doctor."

Mama's head snapped in my direction, her eyes and mouth narrowed into hard, angry slits. "What is the matter with you?" Her voice boomed in the small room. She didn't care that we had an audience. "This is going to cost me a fortune!"

I sat in my seat and stared at the floor as she ranted and paced. I let her words slide right off me without hearing any of them. When we got home, she was going to beat the life out of me. I knew it was coming. I didn't care.

On the way home, there was no conversation around why I stabbed Al. I'd never done anything like that before. This was a new level of aggression for me, and it didn't stop with that one incident. While I never stabbed anyone again, kids who talked badly to me at school were liable to get hit for their trouble. Anyone who said or did something to me I didn't like ended up at the other end of my fist. It was the only way I knew to vent my frustration.

For her part, Mama didn't seem to care why her oldest daughter was suddenly lashing out physically. More often than not, she wasn't around to care.

I don't know where she went during the day. Bob was long gone, and since she'd gotten the settlement check from the VA, Mama wasn't working anymore. My younger brothers and sisters were all in school, and sometimes she'd be there in the morning, but when we got home in the afternoon, the house was empty. Even on Saturdays, she left whenever she woke up and came back when she felt like it. There were no cell phones, so we had no way of getting in touch with her if something happened. She never told me my responsibilities, either; there was no, "Toni, take care of your brothers and sisters, and clean the kitchen before I get home." She just left me to fend for my siblings to the best of my abilities. If she came home and the house was a disaster, she beat us. One of the twins and I looked like my father, and we bore the brunt of Mama's anger.

During one of Mama's disappearances, we didn't have anything to eat. The fridge was empty except for a few random condiment jars. The cupboards held only a loaf of bread. It was already dark outside. My brothers and sisters weren't complaining, but I knew I was hungry, so they had to be, too. I didn't need someone to tell me something needed to be done; I just did it.

I went out the back door and zigzagged across backyards to my cousins' house across the street. Even when Mama was gone, eyes watched our house, ready to report any transgressions. So I moved with great stealth, calculating my every step. My cousins' garage door stood open. My aunt had less money than Mama did, but they'd turned the space into a multipurpose fun room, with a pool table and anything else teenage boys needed for a good time. Her kids never wanted for basic things like dinner.

My cousin Eric sat on the edge of the pool table, cue stick in hand. "What are you doing here?" he asked.

"Mama said to come over and ask for some rice and eggs," I said, looking him in the eye. I was used to asking neighbors to borrow food, and he was family. Usually he gave me whatever I asked for with a smile.

"Your mama ain't told you nothing," he scoffed. "And I'm not giving you nothing. Get out of here."

Shame suddenly burned in my cheeks. I don't know why I lied, and I don't know how he knew it, but I turned around and went home. I remembered how, at Daddy's funeral, Grandma Mary had given me a sandwich with tomatoes and mayonnaise. I improvised. That night, we ate mayonnaise sandwiches for dinner. They became a staple in our diets when there was no food in the house.

There should have been no reason for us to go hungry—my mother was the type of person who would not pay for anything she thought she could get free. In those days, she continually played games with men, telling them her children were theirs to see if they would pay. My sister Erica was only a year younger than I was; Stacy and Tracy were about eight; and LaDonna was going on six years old. As the youngest, LaDonna had the most "daddies," so she had the best of everything. While the rest of us had to alternate—one month the boys got new shoes, the next month Erica and I got shoes—LaDonna got something new every month when her unsuspecting fathers paid the ante. In addition to the fake child support, Mama collected social security and the VA checks every month; if Mama's bank account was low, it was because she was spending money on things we knew nothing about. I realize now she was probably gambling.

One of the guys she tried to con into thinking he was my father was named Donell Jackson. He lived in Kansas City. He worked with a big car company and made big money. She would drive me to his sister's, whom I called Aunt Dot, and they gave me something every time I went there. It was mostly money, which I had to turn over to Mama. I *knew* Erica, the twins, and I belonged to my dad, but we each had three fathers, according to Mama. LaDonna had four or five. At times, my younger siblings didn't know what to believe or who their real father was. It was so confusing.

As soon as I caught on to her scheme, I refused to play along. When she left me with Donell, I cut up so badly she had to come back and get me soon after. My younger siblings were a lot more passive than I was, but as they began to get older and understand what was happening, they also began to resist.

Mama and I butted heads constantly. I questioned everything, acted out in school, and didn't go along with her moneymaking schemes. She didn't know what to do with me. Instead of asking me what was going on, she beat me. Whatever she happened to be holding in her hands turned into a weapon in the blink of an eye. Our altercations boiled to a head one Sunday before church.

"Toni, I'm not saying it again—get dressed and get down here!" Mama shouted down the hallway.

I looked at the ugly dress she'd picked out for me. It was red with busy white squiggles all over it. A big, white, ruffled collar lay against the front. I hated all dresses in general, but this one in particular. "No!" I shouted back. "I won't wear it! It's horrible and ugly."

"Toni, we're going to be late. You put that dress on and shut your mouth."

I stepped out of my room and glared at her. "No."

Mama sent an icy glare down the hallway and shooed my brothers and sisters toward the door. I watched them leave from my bedroom window. I threw the dress on the ground and lay on my bed. For a little while, I felt good about my victory.

Then Mama came back.

The front door slammed shut, startling me. I poked my head out of my bedroom and immediately saw the rage in my mother's eyes . . . and the dead tree branch in her hand.

I dove under the bed, the only place I could think of to hide from her. Mama wasn't a tall woman, but her five-foot-four frame packed at least a hundred and eighty pounds. I wished I had just put on the stupid dress and gone to church.

"Get out here," she ordered as she walked into my room.

Her shoes approached the bed as I cowered against the wall. She grunted softly as she dropped to her hands and knees to see where I was. Her arm shot out and grabbed me. As she yanked me out from under the bed, a bent spring caught the skin over my right eyelid and ripped all the way down to my cheekbone. Bright, hot pain blossomed all along the side of my face. Blood ran down my cheek as she gave me a few licks with the stick she'd brought in from the yard.

"You do what I tell you and don't question it!" she said as she hit me. Then she realized I was bleeding. "Stupid little girl! Look at what you have done."

When she couldn't stop the bleeding, she rushed me to the Natchez Charity Hospital across the bridge, where the ER doctors stitched up my eye. My siblings were still at church, where my mother had left them.

"How did this happen?" one of the doctors asked.

I didn't say anything. I was afraid to even look in Mama's direction. My skin was numb, but I could feel the thread they were using to stitch me up pulling and tugging.

"She was being a bad girl," Mama said, her voice all sweetness and worry. "She was running away from me and wasn't looking where she was going." She continued her lie. I stopped listening. I already knew to her, I was just "bad."

Her story seemed to satisfy the doctors. "Toni was very lucky," they told her. "If that had been any deeper, she could have lost her eye."

When my grandmother heard I'd gotten twenty stitches in my face and almost lost an eyeball, she called the Department of Children and Family Services. I wasn't at home when protective services visited; they must have come while I was at school. When I arrived home one afternoon, I heard Mama talking on the phone in the kitchen.

"I got child protective services called on me. Do you believe it?" she shrieked into the phone. "It's all that crazy girl's fault."

I stopped to listen.

"There's something wrong with her, causing me all this grief."

Me? She was blaming *me?* I couldn't believe what I was hearing.

"She is!" she protested. "She's the cause of all my problems."

I retreated to my bedroom. The now-familiar feeling of anger burned in my stomach. Mama didn't know what to do with me, and I didn't know how to help myself. I sat in my room for days at a time. Mama walked softly until protective services closed the case. Then she sent me to live with my grandma.

"She's the one raising all the sand about you anyway, so let her deal with you," Mama grumbled.

I stepped onto a Greyhound bus by myself in Mississippi. I was traveling to Louisiana with nothing in my hands—no change for an emergency call and no soda, cookies, or chicken to tide me over for the half-day journey. Mama just didn't think that way. I pulled a thin shade down over the window as the bus rolled away from the station. I didn't even look out to see if Mama waved goodbye. She was happy to see me go, and I was more than happy to leave.

Chapter 4

What Goes Around Comes Around

I took a deep breath as the Greyhound pulled away from the station. *Life is going to get better.* My heart sensed it—or at least hoped for it—though my mind refused to believe it.

When Grandma picked me up at the bus station, her face was set in the carefully neutral mask she showed the world. Her voice, though, was warm and worried. "Miss T," she said in the car, using my old nickname, "I am so glad you're here. I hear you've been having problems in school."

"Yes, ma'am," I said, looking at the mighty Mississippi below us as we drove across the bridge toward the city.

"Is it possible you are acting up because you miss your dad?"

The question completely threw me off. Immediately, I thought about that life-altering night with Lil Leo. *I'll kill you and your family.* Those words replayed in my head, and when I thought of them, I felt the same nauseating rush of fear and confusion I had that night. I knew I couldn't tell her the truth, so it was easier to agree than try to come up with a lie.

I shrugged. "I guess."

"Don't worry." Grandma patted my arm as we turned into her neighborhood. "I'll get you the help you need."

I couldn't help smiling as we pulled up to the house. Just seeing the carefully maintained front yard made me breathe a little easier. For all of my childhood, I had come here—all of my family had—when there was nowhere else to go. We always knew we were safe here. This time, I hoped, would be no different.

My grandmother's first order of business was to take me to see a counselor at the sophisticated Jo Ellen Smith Medical Center in Algiers. The state-of-the-art facility housed behavioral and rehabilitation centers, and it was a good half-hour drive from our house. We drove past plenty of doctors' offices and several hospitals on the way to this one, so I knew she'd done her homework trying to find just the right place for me.

Still, as we sat in the waiting room, I wondered what we were doing there. What was I supposed to say to this person?

"Toni Coleman." A white lady, about my grandmother's age, called from the other side of a door.

Grandma and I followed her into her office. The doctor sat in a tall, comfortable chair at the end of a small coffee table. Grandma and I sat on a sofa together. The office was very nice. I propped my shoes up on the table and stared down at my toes while they talked about me as if I wasn't there. The doctor seemed friendly and caring, but I was not about to talk to her. The culture I'd grown up in didn't place any value on professional counseling. When you had problems, you were supposed sweep them under the rug, act like they didn't exist, or talk to your friends or God about them—that's what they were for. Frankly, I didn't have any friends and I was angry at God, but still—under no circumstances would I talk to shrinks.

"I have the information you already provided to my assistant," the doctor said. "But can you tell me in your own words why you think Toni should be here?"

"She's been getting into fights and acting up since her dad died a few years ago," Grandma said, glancing at me worriedly.

"And I see she's recently moved in with you and your husband. Is that right?"

"Yes, ma'am. She was having trouble getting along with her mother."

I squinted my right eye, feeling the slight pull of the healing scar that attested to Grandma's understatement.

"What are you hoping to achieve by bringing her here?"

At that point, I tuned completely out. I didn't care what Mama told her friends. I wasn't crazy and I didn't need to be here.

After my grandmother left, I sat alone in the room with the doctor. I stubbornly held my silent posture while she asked dumb questions and scribbled little notes to herself. I couldn't begin to imagine what she was writing. I surely wasn't giving her anything to work with.

At the end of the session, the doctor looked up at me. "All right, Toni, I'd like for you to come back next week so we can talk some more, okay?"

I got up and walked out of the office without giving her an answer. For six months, every time Grandma said it was time to go, I rode all the way to Jo Ellen Smith, sat across from the doctor for fifty minutes, and refused to say a single word. I didn't want to think about feeling angry, hurt, and unloved.

Living with my grandparents provided brief distractions from the constant mental wars of anger and depression. Every day, Grandma and I took a forty-five-minute commute to her job. Then a van picked me up to take me to Our Lady of Lords Catholic School about fifteen minutes away. At the end of the day, she picked me up from school and we made the forty-five-minute commute home. When we got home, she cooked dinner while I did homework. After dinner, it was time to take a bath and get prepared for the next day. By the time I hit junior high school, I had mastered time management skills and spent most evenings on the phone chatting with friends.

On Saturdays, after my counseling appointments, Grandma took me to dance class and then we went to church. I loved everything about dancing—the music, the steps, dressing up, the people, everything. For a few minutes at a time, I could actually lose myself in the sounds, the rhythm, and the movements. I felt like a star.

After class, the rest of the day was all about Mass. For more than thirty years, Grandma had been a member of St. John's the Baptist Catholic Church on Claiborne Street in downtown New Orleans. Even though Mass was always in Latin, she enjoyed it. Before the ugly church dress altercation with my mother, I hadn't minded going to church. Now I wasn't so sure. I went every week without complaining, following along with the program and intoning the responses and prayers in English—they were ingrained in my head—but I was mad at God. He'd taken my dad and allowed all those bad things to happen to me. If people went to church to say thanks, what did I have to thank Him for? Living with my grandparents was nice, but it almost seemed like too little, too late—a consolation prize after everything I'd endured.

If I'd learned one thing in my short life, though, it was to take nothing for granted. Mama only went grocery shopping after the third of the month, when Daddy's social security and VA checks arrived. While shopping, she bought special things for herself that we weren't allowed to touch. She even hid them from us. Each month, during those precious first few days, my siblings and I gorged ourselves on what we *could* eat. We dared each other to see who could gobble the most pieces of fruit in one sitting. By the end of the month, I was frequently scavenging the neighbors' food supply and relying on those mayonnaise sandwiches.

As cool air leaked slowly from Grandma's open refrigerator, I contemplated the contents. Milk, juice, Coke, Sprite, fresh vegetables, bread, and container after container of leftovers crowded all the shelves. I could have anything I wanted, whenever I wanted it. We always had two full refrigerators of food—one in the kitchen and one in the garage.

"Can I have some of these strawberries?" I called out.

Grandma peeked into the kitchen on her way past. "Toni, you don't ever have to ask for anything in this house. Eat whatever you want. Just make sure you tell Jesse if you take the last of something."

Jesse went grocery shopping every Wednesday, so during the week, I created my own personal grocery list: Twix candy bars, peanut M&M's, the new cereal I saw on TV, potato chips, pickles, pig lips, and anything else I could think of. Sometimes my list came to almost fifty dollars by itself, but Jesse never said a word. Grandma, with her knack for managing money, complained on occasion, but Jesse didn't care. He bought whatever I wanted. Often on Wednesdays, before he left work, he called home to make sure I hadn't forgotten anything. He also called to get my order for dinner on times when he picked up food.

"I'm going to stop and pick up a Po Boy on the way home," he said. "What kind do you want?"

While Jesse made sure I had anything I wanted to eat, Grandma focused on my schooling. She grew up during segregation, but somehow understood the importance of a good education. She earned her high school diploma even though she was required to pick cotton almost every day and walk miles to attend the blacks-only school—at least until St. Francis Catholic School opened to give poor black students a real academic chance. After high school, she went on to become a certified dietitian and worked for the Orleans Parish School Board until retirement. Knowing the obstacles she had overcome drove me to be a high performer. The first quarter I lived with them, I was immediately enrolled in honors classes based on my incoming test scores. Mama didn't put much emphasis on us being good students—she just beat us if we were too bad—and she never helped us with homework.

It took several months to get all of my records released to my new school. The momentary reprieve from my colorful past allowed me to start fresh. By the time my records showed up, I wasn't misbehaving or having regular problems with other students, so the conversations between my teachers and me improved. If something did go wrong, my teachers approached me with questions, not accusations.

"Tell me why this happened, Toni. Is there a better way to solve these types of issues in the future?"

On the two occasions Grandma had to pick me up from school, she used the tactics my teachers did. Instead of yelling at me in the principal's office, like Mama, she tried to understand where I was coming from and why I had done what I did. I responded much better to her style than I did to Mama's style.

No matter where I was, people knew me in school; in Natchez, I was the bad girl, but in New Orleans, I was known for positive things. In Natchez, I was solitary because of my insolent attitude. In New Orleans, I had many friends. Jay, Rochelle, and Shawn were three of my best friends. Jay and I talked every day. We were in band together and both played the drums. On and off, Jay also dated Rochelle and another girl from school named Alicia. Rochelle and Alicia were always arguing over Jay, and you had to ask him monthly which one of them was his current girlfriend. He talked to me whenever he was having issues with either of them. Trying to solve their issues was a regular topic of discussion. I lived on the West Bank, so I never saw them on the weekends, but we talked on the phone every night.

Though I felt I was adjusting well to my new life, Grandma continued taking me to therapy. The questions always started the same, even after six months of me not answering any of them.

"Toni, how are you feeling today?"

I slouched on the couch and stared at the wall across from me. Unbeknownst to Grandma or the counselor, I used most of my time in the counselor's office to replay telephone conversations with my friends in my head. Sometimes I even practiced my latest dance routine, thought out my next grocery list, or made mental notes of things I'd forgotten to tell my friends about the night before. While the counselor tried everything she could to get a reaction out of me, I just daydreamed to avoid the negative emotions I was still harboring.

Shortly after my last doctor's visit, the counselor called my grandmother.

"Mrs. Taylor, based on the information I have and Toni's

behavior during our sessions, I have determined nothing is psychologically wrong with this girl. She just wants her mother's love and doesn't know how to get it. I also believe she misses her brothers and sisters. You should try to take her to Natchez more."

I don't know how she arrived at those conclusions, since I hadn't spoken one word to her during my visits. But they were true. They were just too painful to admit.

Even though my grandparents never verbally said they loved me, I saw and felt it in their actions. With them, I got everything I wanted—including a satellite for my TV. I could order movies or pizza anytime I wanted, and I usually had five pairs of my favorite shoes in different colors, but I was lonely. There was no one to run around with outside. My school friends were all on the East Bank, and Grandma rarely let me out of her sight. At least in Natchez, even if we were hungry sometimes, my siblings and I had each other. For months, I had been so busy focusing on good things I'd been able to hide from all my bad memories, but of course, I couldn't hide forever. In life, unresolved issues always resurface, and usually at the most inopportune moments.

Toward the end of the school year, the conflict between Alicia and Rochelle escalated to a boiling point. They were tired of Jay going between them as he pleased. For weeks, they called each other bad names and talked about fighting while other students fed them lies about what each was saying behind the other's back. I didn't realize, however, that Rochelle was telling kids I was going to help her fight Alicia.

On the last day of school as I walked toward my bus stop, a crowd of people gathered behind me. I didn't pay attention to them until a violent shove between my shoulder blades propelled me off balance and onto the lawn of a nearby property.

"What's this I hear about you helping Rochelle beat me up?"

I turned to see Alicia glaring at me as the mob of kids closed in around us. The mantra of *fight, fight, fight* rang through the air. "I don't know what you're talking about," I said.

"That's not what I hear." Alicia's hands balled into fists at her side. "And now she's turning chicken, so I guess you'll have to fight me yourself."

I had hung up my imaginary boxing gloves a year and a half before. I no longer needed them, or so I thought. I was surprised by Alicia's challenge. Her love triangle with Jay and Rochelle wasn't my problem, but I was not about to back down from a fight. Fighting was one thing I knew how to do.

"Bring it on!" I said.

Alicia lunged at me. I landed a few good punches, her body caving softly to my knuckles. She was shorter, but we were an even match.

"Hey! You girls stop that and get off my grass!" someone shouted.

From the corner of my eye, I caught sight of a lady standing in the doorway of the house whose yard we were tearing up. Alicia looked over and I took the opportunity to charge at her. We fell in a tangled heap.

"I'm calling the police!" The woman's voice faded as she retreated into her home.

I didn't care. I was getting the best of Alicia and venting some of the anger I'd kept pent up for months. As soon as it looked as though I was going to win, a tall girl from our class detached herself from the crowd and joined the fray. She towered over me and outweighed me by at least thirty pounds. I didn't stand a chance against both of them.

The sound of police sirens sent the crowd scurrying away. Alicia and her tag-team partner left me lying on the ground, bruised and irate. *How did I get pulled into this mess?* Rochelle had put me in the middle of her love triangle and then abandoned me. All she had to do was tell me to have my grandmother pick me up, and I wouldn't have been humiliated by Alicia's friend.

"Are you okay?" the woman from the house shouted. When she realized I was bleeding from tussling on the ground, she made a call over to the school where my grandmother worked so she could come pick me up.

"Miss T," Grandma exclaimed, rushing toward me. She put her hands on my face, turning my head first one way and then the other to examine me. "What have you got yourself into?"

"It wasn't my fault!" I burst. "They attacked me! I was just defending myself."

Grandma sighed, apologizing to the woman who lived in the house. "Let's just get you home," she said.

At home, Grandma cleaned my scratches with alcohol and covered the larger ones with Band-Aids. I told her the whole story, and she shook her head silently. She never berated or blamed me.

When Jesse got home, he was fired up to hear about what happened. He was angry, but a little bit proud, too.

"You know why they jumped her?" I heard him crow into the phone to one of his friends. "None of them could have beat her alone, that's why."

After I was all cleaned up, I called Rochelle with vengeance in my heart.

"Hello?" she answered after a few rings.

"Why didn't you tell me you told Alicia I was going to help you fight today?" Anger made my voice shake.

"What?"

"You heard me. And then why did you get your mother to pick you up so you could dodge the fight?"

"Oh, man, I'm—"

"If you had told me, I could have had my grandmother pick me up, too, but instead I got the crap beat out of me by Alicia and one of her friends over your stupid boyfriend. Why did you leave me to fight them alone? You were supposed to be my friend!"

"I'm sorry, Toni, okay? I'm sorry."

She apologized over and over, and Alicia ended up apologizing, too, after she got back together with Jay, but I was livid. I didn't want to hear Rochelle's apologies; I wanted to pay her back.

"Grandma, I don't want to go back to Our Lady of Lords," I told her soon after the fight.

"Why not?"

"I just want to go to a school that's closer to the house and make some friends in the neighborhood."

She agreed. That fall, I started at Ellender Jr. High School on the West Bank. I had never been in a New Orleans public school before. I didn't mind the new environment. I just couldn't shake what Rochelle had done. No matter where I went, the memory of the incident stoked the glowing embers in my heart. It was time to leave Louisiana . . . but not before I paid Rochelle back.

I waited until just before Christmas break; I needed to carefully plan and execute my payback scheme. Once I decided what I was going to do, I called Jay and Shawn and told them about my scheme. Shawn tried to talk me out of it, but Jay agreed he would cover me. My secret payback plot was safe with them; neither told anyone a thing.

"Mama, I'm coming home for Christmas," I said softly into the telephone. I looked over my shoulder to make sure Grandma couldn't hear me. I couldn't bear to tell her I was leaving, but I knew I'd have to get on a bus and out of town as soon as possible; there would be stiff consequences for my scheme. Instead of telling Grandma I wanted to go home, I phoned one of her friends, Ms. Burnett, and asked for a ride to the bus station.

On the last day of school, I cut class and caught a bus over to the East Bank. The ride took three transfers and ninety minutes. I was single-minded and focused, in complete control. Rochelle was going to learn not to betray a friend again.

When I arrived at Our Lady of Lords, I hid behind a tree I knew Rochelle would walk past. As she walked out of the gate, laughing and talking with a group of friends, I grabbed a dead branch from the ground and twisted it in my grip.

"Hi, Rochelle," I said as I stepped directly into her path. We were still on school grounds.

"Toni, hi." An unsure smile lifted the corners of her lips and disappeared when she saw the stick in my hands. Her eyes flicked to the side nervously.

"I bet you thought I forgot about what you did to me at the end of last year, didn't you?"

"What are you talking about?" Her group of friends drifted far behind her. Jay stood on the sidelines, his arms out to block anyone who tried to jump into my fight.

"Well, I didn't forget."

I lit into her with the stick like Mama took after me when

I cut up in school. Caught completely off guard, she tried to fight back, but she was no match for my anger. No one helped her. They all just stood and watched as I let my fury loose on her. When I was finished, she was lying on the ground, bleeding. Now she would feel the same humiliation I did. I walked to the bus stop and never looked back. She didn't care about me, so I no longer cared about her.

Even with the long bus commute, I got home before Grandma. By the time she came in, the phone was ringing off the hook.

"Toni," she called from the kitchen.

I dragged myself out of the bedroom, the lie already on my lips. "Yes, ma'am?"

"That was Rochelle's mother. She said you went back to your old school today and beat up her daughter. What is she talking about?"

"That's crazy, Grandma. I did no such thing. She's lying."

"Rochelle is in the hospital right now. They think she might have a concussion. Toni, tell me the truth, did you have something to do with that?"

"No, Grandma, I've been here all day. That woman is a nut."

The phone rang again. Grandma answered. I waited to see her reaction.

"I don't know what you're talking about," Grandma said into the phone. She looked at me, but I couldn't read her expression. "You go ahead and call the police." After a pause, she responded, "They *should* investigate. If someone hurt your daughter, they should be held accountable. But Toni was here all day. Please keep me posted on Rochelle's condition. If you need anything or if I can help you in any way, please call. These kids," she clucked. "I tell you."

I was on a bus out of New Orleans way before the police ever made it to our side of the river. A few weeks after I got back to Natchez, a detective tried to get a court order to talk to me about the fight. The Natchez judge refused to sign his request.

"If you want to talk to her about this foolishness," the judge said, "wait until she returns to your jurisdiction."

That wasn't going to be any time soon.

Chapter 5

Some Things Never Change

The winter I moved back to Natchez, my mother and I enjoyed a brief honeymoon bliss. For the three years I lived with my grandparents, we only saw each other for a few days at Christmas and Easter when Grandma, Jesse, and I delivered presents to my siblings. Now, suddenly, we were inseparable. I went everywhere with Mama. For the first time in my life, I felt I was part of a mother-daughter team. Most of the time, we hung out with her friends drinking coffee, eating toast, and watching *The Young and the Restless* or *The Guiding Light*. I didn't care what we did, as long as I was with her. In my heart, I knew it wouldn't last—some things never change, no matter how badly you want them to—but I clung to those first few months as best I could.

When the novelty wore off, our relationship disintegrated the way I knew it eventually would. My inquisitive first-born nature constantly triggered her hot buttons. I could usually set her off by asking one simple question: "why?"

"Mama, why do I always have to wear other people's hand-me-downs? Why can't we buy my clothes from the mall? The money you get from Daddy's social security and VA checks is supposed to be used on us. Right? Mama, why can't I have an allowance like the rest of my friends?"

Distance may have temporarily made our hearts grow fonder, but she still didn't know how to deal with me, and I didn't have any patience for her deficient parenting skills. The first time I misbehaved in school, we were right back to square one.

I was in shop class, and my teacher assigned a project of building a wooden chair. I sat with my arms crossed, glaring at him defiantly. "I don't want to build a chair," I said. "I want to build a doll house. Why can't I just build my house?

"Toni, if you don't complete the assignment, I'm going to give you an F," he said. The words were stern, but his voice was weary.

"If it makes you feel better, give me two or three. Who cares?" Since I didn't have Grandma reinforcing the importance of good grades but rather Mama doling out negative reinforcement for bad behavior, I had absolutely no reason to care. I had no future planned, so how could an F impact something that didn't exist anyway?

"The rest of the class is already out in the shop," he added.

"Then you'd best go do what you get paid to do—supervise."

His face reddened as he raised his voice. "You're in dangerous waters, young lady."

"Oh, please. What are you going to do? Send for Mr. Hoffer?" I scoffed, referring to the assistant principal. "Go ahead, call him. I don't care!"

Our disagreement escalated, and Mama was called to come get me. She stormed into the classroom, now filled with other students; I knew I was going to get it even before she opened her mouth. My shop teacher explained the situation, and quick as a flash, Mama was standing next to me, smacking me in the back of the head while she yelled. I tried to duck out of the way of her hands, but she kept up the assault while the rest of class watched. I clenched my teeth. My cheeks burned with embarrassment and anger as my classmates snickered, made low, "Oooh" sounds, and talked about how crazy my mama was.

Once our relationship returned to its naturally sour state, Mama's friend Marianne Gamble offered to take me in every once in a while so we could both cool off. Ms. Gamble was a secretary at the Adams County Legal Aid office in Natchez. She was one of the few friends of Mama's who didn't buy the rationalization I was just a bad kid. Within a few weeks of my first big fight with Mama, I began to spend every weekend with Ms. Gamble and her two children. Tonette, her daughter, was a few years older than I was, and her son Darren was a year younger. I spent so much time with them, people in their neighborhood thought we were siblings.

There was a boy named Calvin who lived on their street whom I liked. He had light skin, like me, and was very good-looking. All the girls were after him. We were both in band, along with another boy named John, who played the drums. While I had my eye on Calvin, John started paying attention to me. He was a few years older and seemed to be a nice country boy, but I was uninterested. His family lived five miles outside of town, and he was completely different from Calvin: his skin was as dark as Calvin's was light, and he rode a motorcycle, which he'd already crashed badly enough to require pins in his leg.

John spent two years walking me to the Gambles' house from school on Fridays and calling me on the phone. Finally, Calvin and I broke up, and he soon started dating another girl. He had her call me on a three-way call to let me know she was the new girl in his life and to beat it. At that moment, John's persistence paid off. Heartbroken and looking for a distraction, I finally agreed to "see" him.

Suddenly, I was talking to him every day, and his favorite topic of conversation was sex. He knew I was a virgin. I was only fourteen years old. We hadn't even kissed, but every time we talked, it was some variation of, "C'mon, Toni. You're so cute—why don't you give me some of that good stuff? A boy has needs."

One day after school, John showed up in my neighborhood. I was outside in the yard, enjoying the warming March weather with my siblings, when I saw him walking down the old train tracks that ran past our house.

"Hi, Toni," he said with a wave. This was the first time he'd been to my house.

"John, what are you doing here?"

He shrugged. "I decided to come to town to see you."

"Oh, really. Why?"

"Is this your house?" he asked, pointing at the one-story behind me.

"Yes."

"Is your mom home?"

"No, and my mama is crazy. That is why I have you walk me to Tonette's on Fridays. If she catches me talking to you, she is going to snap."

"Yeah, well," he grinned suggestively, "she's not here now."

I could see where the conversation was going—all of our conversations ended in the same place. "My brothers and sisters are playing across the street at the park," I said. "And Mama may pop up anytime."

John looked me in the eye, an easy feat since he wasn't much taller than I was. "You know I want to sleep with you—"

"I don't—"

He held up a hand to shush me. "Toni, if you don't give me some, there's a girl just down the street who will."

I stared at him, trying to digest his words. I didn't want to sleep with him, but I'd grown attached to him. I liked having him around and knowing he was going to walk me to the Gambles' house and call me on the phone. Even though I hadn't initially been interested, he made me feel as if I were worth something to him. I didn't want him to disappear.

"Okay, you're taking too long. I'm leaving," he said, his dark eyes watching my expressions carefully.

"Don't leave. I don't want you to go."

He smiled. "Okay, if you want me to stay, you're going to have to give me some. I'm tired of playing these stupid cat and mouse games with you."

Shrugging, I mumbled, "Fine. Whatever." At least he'd stop pressuring me once we'd done it.

I led him through the house, straight back to the bedroom. No one was inside, but like I'd told John, Mama could be back anytime, and who knew when my brothers and sisters would come storming through the door? I lay back on the mattress and waited for him. I didn't know what to expect. In the movies, the man held the woman. They kissed and gasped and whispered how much they loved each other. I didn't think John and I were in love, but then again, how would I know? While my mind raced, I was outwardly calm as John took down my pants and stripped out of his own. With no preamble, he pushed himself inside me and did what he wanted to do; his moves were excited and selfish. I didn't know it was going to hurt; I gritted my teeth against the unexpected pain, hoping it would all be over soon. No one had ever talked to me specifically about sex before.

A few minutes later, it was done. I propped myself up on my elbows as he slid off the bed and pulled on his pants. A small pool of blood collected beneath me. *What is that?* I didn't know having sex could make you bleed.

John caught sight of the growing stain. A proud smirk turned up the corners of his mouth. "I guess that really was your first time." With that, he gathered up his things and left without even saying goodbye or thank you. I had just given him my most precious possession, after his two-year chase, and *this* was how it was going to end?

The bottom of my body felt torn and achy, and now I had to clean up this mess before anyone came home.

Afterwards, our relationship was much the same. We continued to talk, though not every day, and now that he knew where I lived, he came around a little more. At some point, he and Mama crossed paths. She didn't think much of him, but I didn't stop seeing him. Mama couldn't tell me anything about men. What did she know? One of her boyfriends was married, another was ten years her junior, and another lived with his mama. I'd pass on any advice from her. I didn't know much, but I knew something wasn't right about all those men.

By the beginning of summer vacation, I was throwing up every morning and sliding sheets of baking-powder biscuits into the oven daily, to satisfy a fierce craving. I didn't need a doctor to tell me I was pregnant. The signs of a little life growing inside me were everywhere.

I knew I couldn't tell Mama. She would be livid. I wasn't the first in my extended family to get pregnant before marriage, but I was the youngest. I stayed small long enough to cover my belly with regular clothing for months, but I couldn't keep the pregnancy a secret forever. I didn't stop and wonder what would happen when I truly started to show. I was too ignorant to realize the enormity of what this meant for my life; all I could think was at least *now* someone would love me unconditionally. I didn't think about the conversations that needed to happen or the decisions that needed to be made for the future. What future? I lived right in the moment, exactly where I was. All summer, I took care of my brothers and sisters while my own baby developed inside of me.

Just before it was time to go back to school, my mother finally found out. Charles Dottery, a family friend, had dropped by the house, and somehow he instantly knew my secret. He had several kids of his own, so he'd learned to recognize the signs of a pregnant woman. With certainty, he told Mama I was expecting.

In typical Mama fashion, she didn't come to me to have a conversation. She called her psychic instead.

"I'm going to call the house and talk to Toni," the woman said. "I'll be able to tell whether she's pregnant or not."

Sure enough, the phone rang one afternoon and Mama told me it was for me. After we talked for a few minutes, I passed the phone back to Mama.

"Yeah," the woman said, "Toni is definitely pregnant."

Mama's first reaction was extreme. "You are having an abortion," she yelled. "That's it—no ifs, ands, or buts about it!"

"No!" I shouted back at her, horrified. "I am not killing my child."

"I knew that boy was good for nothing! I told you I didn't want him coming around here. I told you I didn't like him.

Why are you always causing me trouble? I am too young to be a grandmother."

She was crazy if she thought I wasn't keeping my baby. My baby would love me, something she seemed incapable of doing. She could forget about this baby going down anybody's tube.

John's parents, Freddie and Inez Woodfork, weren't thrilled by the idea of being grandparents either, but they didn't immediately demand I kill our unborn child. John and I decided to make the best of the situation; we agreed to stop "seeing" each other and officially start dating. Years later, I would find out he told his parents the baby wasn't his and I'd been sleeping around. Because of Mama's wild reputation, they believed him.

When school started in the fall, it was impossible to hide my belly. I walked down the hallways in my Walmart clothes, which had always branded me as poor even though we shouldn't have been, while everyone stared. My defiant stride eventually became a waddle, my ankles swollen and painful. The heavier, more obviously pregnant I became, the more judgmental the stares turned. My classmates and teachers alike didn't bother hiding their contempt. Whispers flew whenever I walked by, and now—unlike the old days—I couldn't just hit someone. I was vulnerable in a way I had never been before, and it was as if everyone knew it. One by one, my former friends drifted away as their parents found out about my condition. Not only was I a bad girl, I was now a bad influence. By November, I walked the halls alone. I was fifteen, eight months pregnant, and except for Tanya Gee—a girl who lived in the next subdivision—friendless. The hormones racing through my system made me feel the anger and depression much more acutely. I had nowhere to turn.

My younger sister, Erica, picked up on how negatively the insults affected me, even though I struggled not to show it.

"You're just a pregnant b—h!" The word rang harshly in my ears as she shouted during one fight. "You will never amount to anything!" She slammed the bedroom door in my face. The look of triumph in her eyes told me I could no longer conceal the terrible emotions I was feeling. I was worthless, shamed, depressed, and hopeless. I couldn't see how the future would be any better than the present, and I had lost any will to wait and see. The Toni of my past—incensed, shrill, never one to back down from a fight—was gone. In her place was a girl who just wanted to be gone.

· · ·

After I took the pills that quiet afternoon, my muscles relaxed one by one as I sank into sleep. I didn't wake up until Mama grabbed my shoulders, lifting me from the bed as she shook me.

"Did you take these?" she yelled, one hand around the pill bottle. "Come on, Toni, wake up—what did you do?"

My head flopped back and forth in a nod, and the next thing I knew I was writhing in pain in the back of Mama's car. I don't remember anything about the drive, but I imagine her head was consumed with what would happen if the Department of Children and Family Services found out. Maybe it's cynical, but I suspect she was speeding to the hospital as much to save herself as to save me. I can't say for certain, because we never talked about it. Not once.

When I woke up, the hospital room was cold, and my stomach ached from being pumped. *I'm still here,* I thought. The saga had not ended, and I was sure there was more of it to come.

I went to mandated counseling for a while, but the experience wasn't much different from when Grandma had taken me to therapy in Louisiana. I wasn't comfortable talking, even though looking back, I desperately needed to. So I sat on a couch with my mouth shut. These sessions didn't last more than a couple of months. You can't help someone who doesn't want to be helped.

· · ·

Early in the afternoon on December 16, 1985, I went into labor, and the nightmare continued for twenty-four hours.

I'd had a few false starts, so at first Mama didn't believe it was time—especially since the baby's due date wasn't until the 25th. As a result, I labored at the house until the next morning; part of me was convinced she was still punishing me.

"Oh, God," I screamed, doubling over as another contraction hit me. *"Help me!"*

"Come on, Toni, let's go," Mama finally said, rounding me up toward the door.

John was at our house but chose not to go with us to the hospital. "I hate you!" I shouted at him, nearly retching with the pain. "This is all your fault!"

"Don't pay her any mind," Mama told him. "She doesn't mean what she's saying. Now, come on, Toni, go!"

I yelled at John some more as we left the house, ignoring the hurt in his eyes. I thought of the first time we had sex. Was that the day I got pregnant? It didn't matter now, because the baby was coming and it was all I could do to hang on.

We picked up Aunt Sarah on the way. Any time anyone in the family went to the hospital, Aunt Sarah was a permanent fixture. She was with you from beginning to end, making sure everybody did their jobs—the doctors, nurses, cleaning staff, and you. By this time, my contractions were only five minutes apart. I felt like they were ripping me in half.

"You can do this, baby!" Aunt Sarah coached me in the car. "We're almost there. Just breathe like I showed you!" She took deep breaths and I desperately tried to mimic her, but my head was spinning from the pain. I almost believed the baby was going to force its way out right there in the car. I just wanted relief, something to help me not hurt so much.

It took an hour and a half to get to Kuhn Memorial Hospital, a state hospital in Vicksburg. My dad had left us with insurance, but Mama was too cheap to pay the two-hundred and fifty dollar co-pay. Besides, I needed to learn a lesson through humiliation, so we were going to a hospital for poor people.

At Kuhn, people invaded my room whenever they felt like it. I hated it. Though I shared a bedroom with my sisters at home, they typically didn't spend as much time in there as I did. Here, several other girls occupied the room with me, our beds separated by drab curtains. Mama didn't want Aunt Sarah in the delivery room, so she had to wait outside in the visitors' area. I would have rather had my aunt with me. Mama was neither comforting nor helpful but a presence that grated on my nerves. All I wanted was to be left alone, but because I'd downed a bottle of pills just a month before, no one trusted me. Since I was a minor, I wan't legally allowed to make my own decisions.

"Would you like us to give her something for the pain?" one of the nurses asked my mother as I moaned.

"No. Don't give her anything," Mama said firmly. "I want her to have it natural. She needs to understand what she has done. If she wants to act grown, let her be grown. Don't give her a thing. I mean it."

I felt every moment of labor, and everyone on my floor knew it. Tears poured from my eyes as I gasped and cried, dilating from centimeter to centimeter.

One of the nurses twitched aside the curtain and hissed at me. "There is a ten-year-old girl in one of the beds across the room who was *raped*, and she's not making half as much noise as your fast-tail behind."

My mouth fell open. I was about to cuss her flat-out when another contraction stole my breath. How could someone I didn't even know be so mean? The constant agony didn't let me linger on those thoughts for long. Shortly after noon, exhausted and out of my mind with pain, I finally gave birth to my first child. Mama named my new baby doll Candes.

Part 2

Activating the
Power Within

Chapter 6

It's Time for a Change

It was clear from the beginning Candes wasn't mine. I'd looked forward to having her because I knew someone would finally love me unconditionally, but when we got home, it was *Mama* who had a baby—not me. Mama fed her, slept with her, and took care of her every day. John and I didn't have to do anything.

After the holiday break, school returned to normal. It seemed as though Christmas break had given all the kids amnesia about me being pregnant; they all treated me as they had before I began showing. "Stay out of Toni's way unless you want to get into something." What they didn't know was the hard edges of the old, defensive Toni were starting to wear away.

Mama didn't let Candes out of her sight until she was three months old. After that, John picked us up every evening after work, and we went to his parents' house. Around ten o'clock, he drove us home, and Candes went right back to Mama. Part of me was glad; when Candes woke up screaming in the middle of the night, I wasn't the one who had to get up to comfort her. Besides, it left John and me free to focus on our relationship.

I wasn't thinking about having any more kids when John surprised me one day.

"Toni, we should have had a son first," he said seriously, as if we could plan it. "Now we have to have a son."

"Are you kidding me?" I laughed. "I don't want more kids anytime soon!"

But I couldn't remember to take my birth control pills—I skipped two or three days in a row and then picked up where I left off. Since the true responsibilities of raising a kid weren't ours, there was no incentive to be more responsible. Within six months, I was pregnant again.

I'd had terrible morning sickness and a tough emotional pregnancy with Candes, but this time was different. This time, the first sign of a new child growing inside me was my clothes feeling snug. When school started again in the fall, everyone except Mama questioned the wisdom of me having another child so quickly. I didn't let their comments faze me one bit; I just didn't care. I was grown, pregnant, and in control of my life, and there wasn't anything anyone could do about it!

Then one day, I was watching TV at John's parents' house. John wasn't home, his mother was making dinner, and Lisa, his little sister, was in her room playing with Candes. Lisa's soft cooing and the baby's high giggle drifted through the air. John's father stopped in the living room.

"Hello, Mr. Woodfork," I greeted him without looking up from the TV. After returning from work, he usually continued on to his bedroom to take his shower and get ready for dinner. This evening he had something else on his mind.

"Toni," he said in his low, calm voice, "I hear you are pregnant again."

"Yes, sir," I said slowly.

"If you keep going at this rate, by the time you are twenty-one, you and John will have seven kids." He gave me a concerned, fatherly look before walking out of the room.

That shook me. Come again? *Seven kids?* Me? No *way* was I having seven kids! I knew firsthand how hard it was to grow up in a household where there wasn't enough to go around. Whether it was for new clothes, shoes, groceries, or Mama's love, I always felt like a beggar. Oh, no—I was not going to let that happen to *my* children.

I wasn't the only one worried about providing for a family. Shortly after John found out I was pregnant for the second time, he decided to leave Natchez and relocate to Texas. Since commercial shipping transportation had taken the place of steamboats, you couldn't make any real money in Natchez unless you were a trained professional. Even though John had been working at the local sawmill for a few years, he only made three hundred dollars a week—not nearly enough to take care of two kids and me. I didn't know what kind of job he had in mind, but Texas seemed to be the Promised Land. The man I loved, the father of my babies, was leaving us. I was devastated. How was I going to adjust from seeing him every day to not even knowing when I'd next *hear* from him? It was all I could do to wrap my mind around the change.

John left with little fanfare. We hugged goodbye to a chorus of his promises to come back for us, and then my attention turned toward Candes. I wanted to spend more time with her, to come in from the streets and be the responsible mother I wished Mama had been. John would return for us eventually, and I wanted to be a good wife and parent when he did.

When my attitude shifted in this way, Mama and I launched into regular disputes over how to care for my daughter. The pediatrician told us not to give Candes rice cereal until she was four to six months old. Mama took it upon herself to start feeding her rice at two weeks old. By the time my daughter was old enough for cereal, Mama had moved on to potatoes and other solid foods. I wasn't happy with how chubby *my* baby was getting, and I told her so.

"I am the only parent in this house!" Mama shouted after a heated argument.

I realized I would never be Candes' mother while living under my mother's roof. Just as I always did when things weren't going my way in Natchez, I packed my bags—and, this time, my baby—and headed straight for New Orleans.

As soon as I arrived, Eliza Brooks Taylor laid down the law.

"Toni, you can't bring *any* more children into this house," Grandma said. "Candes is fine, the one you're going to have is fine, but if you have any more kids, you are going to have to find someplace else to live. Miss T, you can't eat those kids, and I told you that boy doesn't mean you any good. Do you understand me?"

I opened my mouth to protest, but she kept talking.

"You also have to hurry up and get your school stuff done. You're going to need a high school diploma to get a good job."

I thought about it for a few minutes. "Okay, Grandma, it makes sense." Then a thought occurred to me. "But I need you to sign for me to have my tubes tied. I can't remember to take birth control like I'm supposed to."

"Sure, honey, that's fine."

Grandma always had a way to get me to do what she wanted; if Mama had tried the same conversation, it would have ended in shouting, but Grandma was a wise woman. She enrolled me in an accelerated education program through

John Ehret High School. Most of us in the satellite program had one kid already, and no one knew I was pregnant at the time. I didn't get nearly as big as I had with Candes, so my condition remained a secret until graduation. Once again, leaving my mother's house helped me buckle down and get to work. We all settled into our latest new normal. Candes went to daycare, Grandma and Jesse went to work, and I went to school and doctor's visits.

Dr. Jones had an office a half a mile from Grandma's house. I told him right away about my plan to get my tubes tied.

"Seventeen is too young," he told me. "You're just going to have to keep taking the pill, sweetheart."

"Doc, you have to help me out. If I have any more kids, I won't be able to stay at my grandmother's anymore. I can't leave her with a bunch of kids." I thought of Grandma's serious face when I'd arrived. There was no doubt in my mind—she meant business. If I had more kids, I wouldn't have anywhere to go. My cousins, the Hugheses, were in Natchez, and God knew I needed to stay far away from that town. Nothing good for me happened there.

I pressed Dr. Jones every time I went in for a checkup. I didn't want to leave anything to chance.

"Listen," he finally said to me one day. "After this one is born, if you make it for a year without getting pregnant, I will tie your tubes."

"Deal."

Shortly after I received my diploma, Aunt Sarah came down to New Orleans to be with me for the birth. The entire experience was easier than the first time, simply because my mother wasn't there. As soon as I was in a bed at West Jefferson Memorial Hospital, the anesthesiologist gave me an epidural. My son John was born on February 26, 1987, at 2:10 p.m.

Aunt Sarah stayed for a month to help out, but I was on my own after that. Parenting responsibilities for Candes and Lil John were all mine since Grandma and Jesse both worked. As soon as John was old enough for daycare, Grandma pushed me into junior college. She didn't know much about college except it would keep me busy and help me become more successful. Unenthused, I enrolled anyway to keep Grandma happy.

My first attempt at higher education only lasted one semester. Through school, I met other girls my age who were more interested in socializing and partying than studying. We weren't old enough to get into adult clubs, but New Orleans had several teen clubs not far from Grandma's house. On the weekends, after I put my children to bed—I never left before they were tucked in for the night—we headed out to party until five or six o'clock in the morning. As long as I wasn't hurting anyone or getting into trouble, Grandma didn't care. She stayed up until eleven o'clock or midnight to make sure the kids didn't need anything. She knew I needed to have a life.

At this point, Big John and I were still together, but he was in Texas and I was in Louisiana. We had been apart for over a year; he hadn't even met the son I'd named after him. I so desperately wanted to be Mrs. Toni Woodfork and for my children to grow up with their father. However, though our conversations regularly drifted toward marriage, John refused to take the next step. In the back of my mind, I began to wonder if I wasn't good enough for him. *Why doesn't he want to marry the mother of his children?*

"None of the men in my family get married before thirty," he told me repeatedly. He wanted me to move to Texas with him without putting a ring on my finger. Mama was against it, so we planned my move in secret. I was blinded by love.

John came to pick us up in New Orleans for Memorial Day weekend to go to Natchez; I knew when we left my grandma's house I wasn't coming back. I didn't tell her I was leaving for Texas because I knew she would miss Candes and John. It always seemed easier to leave first and apologize later.

A few days after our reunion glee, when we spent as much time as we could in bed together, John drove the kids and me to Mama's house. We unloaded the car, left the kids with Mama, and got back in the car.

"Get out, Toni," John said. His tone was pleasant, conversational.

"Why? Did you leave something inside?"

"I'm going out with my friends."

"John, we've been apart for a year and a half," I objected. "Why can't I go with you?"

His face darkened as he glanced toward me and then forward again, toward the road. "You just can't. Get out of the car."

I gave him a beseeching stare. "Please? I miss spending time with you."

"Get *out* of the car," he said again, the edges of his words sharp.

"No. Why can't I go? I just want to be with you."

Before I knew what was happening, John's hand flew through the air and smacked me in the face.

I was shocked. I was only eighteen and had never been hit by a boyfriend before. Tears pooled in my eyes as I jumped out of the car, and my chest stung with heartbreak and confusion. John had never hit me—not even close. Why now? Why didn't he want to spend time with me? Didn't he still love me?

It didn't take long for surprise and sadness to turn into anger. Mama's words came back to me: "You shouldn't be going to another state with him unless you're married."

As much as I hated to admit it, she had a point. In Texas, I wouldn't have any family around. What would happen if he hit me again? Where would I go?

When my relatives found out he had hit me, conversations with them turned to questions about whether this was the right relationship for me. I was already mad about the slap, but now they were putting doubts into my head about the whole relationship. John dropped by the house several times that weekend, but I refused to see him.

When his vacation was over, he called to say he was heading back to Texas.

"I'm sorry," he said for the third or fourth time. "I don't know what got into me. You know I've never hit you before, and I'll never do it again. I promise."

My heart melted, but my resolve didn't. I still loved him and wanted to be with him, but I was dead set against leaving with him now.

"Please, Toni," he said softly. "Just come to Texas with me. You'll see. I'll be different."

The hiss of static crackled through the phone line. John's breathing carried all his promises, trying to undo the damage left by the new doubts in my head. "I'm not going with you," I finally told him.

John left Natchez without seeing me again. Instead of focusing on the problem of still wanting to be with him, I turned my attention toward my children. As usual, life in Natchez never went well for me. Mama and I couldn't agree on how to raise Candes and Lil John, so conflict arose again. I packed my bags and headed back to New Orleans. Life was always better there, and my grandparents' door was always open for me.

John called me frequently from Texas. At first, I refused to talk to him. I met new guys at the mall or at clubs when I went out with my cousins Chanell and Anita. Because of what had happened to me when I was younger, I never let men I didn't know around my children. Most didn't even know I had kids unless the subject came up in a general discussion. There weren't many young men my age interested in parenthood, so I only had two serious relationships during this stretch in Louisiana. In between, I continued talking to John. I was still upset he'd hit me, but our conversations were always full of his promises. He apologized. He cried. He swore nothing like it would ever happen again.

Eventually, his words started to wear me down, and instead of luring me to Texas, he offered to move back to Natchez so we could be a family again. I hopped at the chance. I did miss him, and I didn't have any better options in New Orleans. The kids and I headed back to Natchez.

I was determined this time would be different. Instead of moving in with Mama, I found an apartment for the three of us. It was located above a restaurant and across the street from Holy Family (formerly St. Francis), our family church. Though I didn't have a car, my cousin Mona gave me a ride anywhere I needed to go—except to John's house. She refused to drive through Dead Man's Curve to get to his place, so John visited us when he could. The kids and I had our own kitchen, living room, a balcony, and a bedroom, but we shared communal washrooms with the other tenants. Within a few months, I started looking for a new place where we wouldn't have to clean the bathtub and toilet with Clorox every time we wanted to use them.

We finally settled into a duplex apartment in Broadmoor, the country neighborhood where John's parents lived. They were only three streets away, and John spent most of every day with the kids and me.

The new apartment had two bedrooms and its own bath. Our next-door neighbors were a couple with eight children. They had three bedrooms between the ten of them. You could tell they were struggling, but they were good people. The husband and wife got along well and respected each other. At the time, I was collecting my dad's social security and VA checks; and I had a bunch of money in a trust I would get when I turned twenty-one. Cash was not a problem. I didn't need to work. My days were consumed by playing with the kids, talking on the phone, cleaning house, cooking dinner—I was a regular stay-at-home mom.

Schedules and routines didn't mean anything to us. The kids and I lived in the moment. We got up when we wanted to, ate when we were hungry, and went to bed when we were tired. But now since we lived in the country, Mona could no longer pick us up. Dead Man's Curve, which she felt lived up to its name, was a real issue for her. I had to rely on John more, which meant keeping track of his schedule. It didn't take long for his promises to disintegrate.

When John wasn't home by four or five o'clock, I usually had a few questions for him. My questions led to arguments, especially when I knew he wasn't telling me the truth about where he had been.

"Why'd it take you so long to get home tonight?" I asked. It was six.

John sighed, brushing past me toward the bedroom without answering.

"Where were you?"

"I got off work late, Toni," he said. "Leave me alone."

But I couldn't. I was required to let him know where I was; why didn't it work both ways?

I followed him into the bedroom, where he was taking off his shirt. "You never work this late. You always get off at three."

"Toni, I'm not talking about this anymore. Drop it."

My heart was pounding, arms crossed as I stared at him. He was lying, and I knew it. Nothing had changed from when we were younger when he fooled around on me. The man didn't know the definition of the word monogamy.

"John, you—"

With one step forward, John smacked me across the mouth. I gasped, raising a hand to my throbbing lips. My shaking fingers came away without blood, but my ears were ringing from shock. All I could think was, *He promised he'd never hit me again!*

John didn't say a word—just shook his head in disgust and walked out of the room. I heard the apartment door open and slam shut behind him. Night fell as I sat on the edge of the bed, utterly alone.

From that point on, our arguments devolved into physical fights at least every other month. I learned early on he became more aggressive whenever I hit him back. You'd have thought I was another guy on the street, not the mother of his kids. By our fourth or fifth fight, I just covered my head and face to protect myself from his vicious blows and kicks.

Inevitably, he stormed out the side door, and then my neighbor came to check on me.

"Is everything okay?" she'd ask as the door swung open.

"I'm fine."

"This isn't good," she'd tell me. "No one should be hitting on you, especially your boyfriend. What are you teaching your daughter? What is he teaching your son? You have to stop this. Your kids are going to grow up confused, and he will lash out at them at some point. These types of abusers eventually evolve to abusing kids, too. Hitting is always about maintaining control over someone or something."

I knew what she was saying was true, but we were locked in a destructive cycle. He beat me, I got mad, cried, refused to see him for a few days or weeks, and then I started to miss him. He'd call and keep trying to see me, eventually wearing me down.

"I don't know why I do this," he said over the phone. "I'm sorry. I've never hit anyone else before. I don't know why I get so upset with you. If you'd just do what I ask, this wouldn't happen."

Somehow, he always found a way to blame me. I would give in, and we started the cycle of abuse all over again.

Natchez was a small town, and anytime someone saw me with a black eye or busted lip, the word got back to my family. Occasionally, one of my cousins tried to talk to me, but I never listened. I wasn't ready to give up on my little family. It wasn't until my cousin LindaKay put it to me candidly that my eyes opened.

We were in the car with her sisters, Mona and Lorraine. Mona was driving me home from the doctor. I always seemed to get sick after John and I fought. The doctor gave me a prescription for Zantac to calm my stomach, but it didn't calm the hurricane in my mind.

"Toni," LindaKay said, "you don't have to hide anything from us. If you like the way John treats you, then guess what? We love it."

It was her way of telling me she was tired of dealing with me sneaking around with John when we were supposed to be broken up, then running to one of them in times of desperation. On the one hand, I wanted to do the right thing and break away from this unhealthy relationship; on the other, I wanted my children to be raised by their father. They needed *both* of us. But LindaKay's words struck a chord with me. I didn't like the way John treated me, not at all.

One day, we were at his parents' house with the kids. Once again, John wanted to go out without me and told me to stay there until he got back.

"No way," I said, crossing my arms. "I'm not going to sit here while you go out with your little women. I know what you're doing in the street. My friends come back and tell me. If you want to go out, I'm going home."

"The kids should spend some time with my parents."

"Fine. They can stay here, but I'm leaving." I got up and walked out of the house. Before I got halfway to my apartment, I heard tires crunch the asphalt behind me and then come to a stop. I didn't turn around, not even when the car door opened and slammed shut. Then John jumped me from behind. Right there, in the middle of the street, my boyfriend started beating me. I fell to the ground, curling into a ball to protect myself, but he was totally enraged.

"Who are you to disrespect me in front of my family?" he shouted. "That's the problem! You don't understand your place!" He ripped my shirt off and continued to hit and kick me everywhere. My breasts hung out for everyone to see, my dignity stripped away.

"Hey!" A man rushed from his front door. "Take this mess off our street. We don't want fighting around here—we have kids here. What kind of examples are you?"

John glared at me, his dark eyes showing nothing but rage. Without a word, he got into the car and drove away. The man who'd stopped him went back inside without checking to see if I was okay. He'd done his part. As I lay there, shaking and half-naked, I realized living outside the city limits with no immediate family nearby was a very bad choice. It was time for a change.

Mama happily took me in at her new house—this way, she would have control over my money again. I had my own room, but I couldn't spend all day in the house. She drove me nuts, and her new husband, William, liked young girls. It didn't take long for me to get tired of fending off his sexual advances.

I started working at McDonald's to occupy some of my time. The manager, Brian, and I were good friends, but that soured when his girlfriend started working at our restaurant. I wasn't one to keep quiet when I saw favoritism unfairly affecting the rest of us. One Saturday, I'd had enough of always being stuck in the back drive-through, where I had to wash dirty dishes that piled up every hour, while she stood at the front registers smiling in his face. I called him on it, and he tried to explain his behavior away. When that failed, he tried an ultimatum.

"Toni, you either get back in drive-through or go home. And if you leave, don't bother coming back."

I glared at him. "Fine. I won't." I stomped out of the restaurant and went straight home.

My brothers and sisters were in the front room watching TV when I stormed through on the way to my room. Mama was talking to someone in the beauty salon she ran at the back of the house. I ignored their voices at first, but then I realized who the other woman was: Vivian.

Over the years, I'd heard Mama cut Vivian down for thinking she was better than other people were. When Vivian's first marriage fell apart, she had to adjust to a new, less luxurious lifestyle. Mama was thrilled about Vivian's fall. The fact these two were having a conversation without any cussing or fussing piqued my interest.

"Praise God," said Vivian. "I've been going to First Pentecostal Church in Woodville for two years; it has changed my life." She noticed me hanging out in the hallway and smiled. "Why don't you come to church with me tomorrow, Toni?"

Mama looked directly at me. Smirking, she said, "She isn't going to nobody's church."

God and I hadn't been on speaking terms in at least four years, but I was curious. From what I could tell, Vivian wasn't at all a snob. What could she have gotten into that turned her into such an overly nice person?

"Okay," I said, surprising Mama and myself.

When Vivian picked me up the next day, I wasn't sure what to expect. I rode in the back of her car with her daughter Vivica. A man named Frank, another person Vivian wanted to introduce to God, rode in the front. Vivian kept up a stream of lighthearted chitchat throughout the thirty-mile drive.

My mother's whole family is Catholic. Every service is like the last, and after a few of them, even little kids know the routine by heart. As we pulled into the parking lot, I could already hear the noise inside the church. The steady thump of drums and the deep reverberation of an organ filled my ears. Even so, I was not prepared for the chaos that waited inside.

People were dancing and shouting, sweating and fanning themselves with programs. They looked as if they were having the time of their lives in church. I stared in amazement, unable to comprehend what was happening. *These folks are crazy!* The pastor appeared out of nowhere with a big smile on his face. He said something to me, but I shrank away. I wanted to go home but couldn't. I was stuck there as long as Vivian stayed.

After more singing and dancing, amidst shouts of "Halleluiah!" "Praise God!" and "Amen, brother!" the pastor stood to give his sermon. He wasn't a tall man, but his presence filled the front of the church. The timbre of his voice spoke to the years he'd spent singing before he was saved.

"Take a look at the life you're living." He looked out over his crowd, waiting for us to examine ourselves. "Is what you're doing working for you?"

Suddenly, I felt he was speaking directly to me.

"If not," he said, letting his words hang, "maybe it's time for a change. Give God the opportunity to make a difference in your life."

His words echoed in my head for the rest of the forty-five minute sermon. During the ride home, I couldn't stop thinking about the message. Those people seemed crazy, but could reconnecting with God help me make the changes I needed in my life?

The thoughts swirling around in my head were new—and hopeful. I went back to church with Vivian every so often;

however, I was only eighteen. I still wanted to party. This church thing was going to be a slow process for me, if it happened at all.

Since John and I were somewhat over, I started talking to other guys. I didn't see any problems with it until three of them showed up at Mama's house to see me at the same time. I was only sleeping with one of them, but all three thought of me as their girlfriend.

The first one showed up in the afternoon. We sat in the living room and talked for an hour. When the second guy knocked at the door, I knew I had to be more careful about what I said, but there wasn't yet a problem. They knew each other but there were two other teenage girls in the house—I figured they'd each assume the other was there to see one of my sisters.

I made it a game in my head and was having a good ole' time. I knew they were both there for me, but they were clueless. I was now officially a player, and I was finally giving guys a taste of their own medicine. It was exciting. I settled into the sofa and watched the game unfold.

Some time later, I looked out the window. The third guy's car was headed straight for the house. At first, I thought my eyes were playing tricks on me. *He said he had to work today.* As reality set in, my heart skipped a beat. This guy was an absolute nut. He was older and extremely confrontational. His reputation alone scared other guys out of messing with his girlfriends—no way would he sit in the living room with two other guys and chat politely. Within minutes, he'd figure out they weren't here for my sisters, and then things would get nasty. I could hear Grandma's voice in my head: *You got yourself into some real stuff here, Miss T. What about those kids?*

His car pulled up to the curb and stopped. I had to get out of there or someone was going to get hurt. I could feel it. As his door opened, I dove off the sofa.

"I have to go," I said to the other two.

I dashed out the front door as fast as I could. A realization slapped me in the face—if I had been sleeping with all of them I would have seen the connection earlier—despite my desire to run in the other direction, I was following right in my mother's footsteps. The light bulb came on: *life isn't a game*. If I got hurt, what would happen to my kids? Would they grow up with my mother? Would they be taken away because I was playing stupid, childish games, not realizing there were consequences?

It was definitely time for a change.

Chapter 7

The Past Does
Not Define Us

After the incident with the three guys, my consciousness awakened. Grandma had been telling me all along I needed to get more serious about life, especially for my kids, while Vivian constantly reminded me of all the untapped potential I had on the inside; but it took one moment that could have gone very badly to make me *think*. It was a critical time in all of our lives. What did the next five or ten years look like for us? What was I creating for the little people I had brought into this world? I didn't want my kids going through the things I went through. All the transitions, the popping up and moving from place to place whenever I didn't get my way, needed to stop. In order to change their lives, I needed to change me. It was time to get focused and serious about the future.

The first thing I did was look at the people around me. Who had it together? Who didn't? What role models could I emulate, and what types of people should I avoid? My friends were concerned with partying, having a good time, worrying about what to wear, getting caught up with all the latest fashions, getting their hair done every week—foolishness, all of it.

I realized early on if I changed my habits, a lot of folks I hung out with would choose to spend their time elsewhere. I was willing to make the sacrifice, but it was easier said than done.

Pine Street was the easiest route from Mama's house to my aunt Sarah's or Big John's house. After eight o'clock each night, the activity buzzing down Pine tempted me to go out and have fun. Every single time I drove down that street, someone tried to flag me down.

"Toni! Hey, Toni!" they called, laughing and stumbling. "Park the car and come over here!"

After a few failed attempts at being responsible, I started to take the long way around from my aunt's house to Mama's house. Still, a small city like Natchez didn't offer many alternatives, and the temptation didn't go away. After all, I knew where all my friends were, and in moments of boredom or frustration, I still thought, *I'm only 18, I have plenty of time to change—why not?* But there were three big reasons why not: Candes, Lil John, and me. I needed a clean break, especially from the latest pervert mama had married. He was about five feet nine inches, with a raspy voice and decrepit face. I was old enough—and he was skinny enough—to keep his advances at bay, but I didn't want my children anywhere near him.

I moved to New Orleans one more time. Even though I'd partied there, too, it was easier to resist because Grandma's house was a twenty-minute drive from the nearest teen club.

"I'm not moving out of here until I'm married," I told Grandma and Jesse. I intended to keep that promise. Of course, no one believed me.

The first thing I did in New Orleans was track down a church. Although I still wasn't quite sure how I felt about God, I thought if I filled my schedule with good activities, at least I wouldn't be as tempted to go out and party. Vivian recommended the First Pentecostal Church of the Westbank. I had gone to the same type of church with her, but this one was much more sophisticated, maybe even a little snooty.

The congregation was predominantly white and made up of businesspeople: entrepreneurs, attorneys, dentists, chiropractors, and other highbrow types. The pastor had been a corporate executive before he started the church, and he had high standards of excellence. It was the most prestigious, architecturally beautiful building on the West Bank. It felt like a cathedral inside, with soaring ceilings and dappled sunlight streaming through stained glass. The choir stand held at least a hundred people.

The first three or four months I was in New Orleans were consumed with trying to understand what I believed—not just about God but all the values and teachings of First Pentecostal Westbank. I had a lot to learn about making lasting change and being a productive member of society. I'd never been able to break away from Big John or the partying for sustained periods of time. Just maybe, if I put all of myself into what the church taught, I could break the cycle.

I took my new goals seriously. Sunday mornings started with Sunday school at ten o'clock, followed by service from eleven to twelve-thirty, and evening service lasted an hour and a half. On Tuesday nights, I went to small group meetings, and Wednesdays were scheduled for bible study. Since I was under twenty-one, I also went to youth service on Friday nights. A separate youth church, a miniature replica of the grand structure, stood behind the main building. Prayer sessions every weekday at six a.m. helped me set a routine. When I got home, it was time to get the kids ready for school.

There was another session in the evenings, and occasionally I dropped in for the ten o'clock women's prayer session.

Outside of church, I spent time with friends from the congregation. There were gatherings at people's houses at least once a month for fellowship and chitchat. People shared things they were struggling with and gave each other advice on how to overcome those issues. My self-destructive habits—drinking, partying, and running around with boys—were all easy to overcome once I filled my days with constructive activities. Unbeknownst to me, I had been hurting myself more than anyone else had, including Andre, Penny, Pam, and Lil Leo. They had become irrelevant to my life, even if I still needed to deal with deeply buried emotional scars.

I hadn't realized it, but I couldn't heal one hundred percent without examining those wounds, and I wasn't willing to tackle them yet. Still, once I exercised some control over the cussing, the drinking, the partying, and the boyfriends, I automatically started to feel better. I didn't wake up hungover or, worse, still intoxicated. I didn't cuss people out at the drop of a hat. I didn't sleep around with guys to make myself feel better. I moved beyond thinking of myself as the bad girl, the bad influence, and that felt like a big deal. Sometimes the best we can do is work with what we know at the time.

Dad's social security and VA checks were still coming in, and the lump sum was still sitting in the bank. Although I didn't have to work, it was a common value at First Pentecostal Westbank. My church believed you should work if you were able. Accepting any type of government aid was out of the question. On top of that, they liked to keep young, impressionable people busy. Keeping busy was the key to preventing kids from making bad choices. That was where Brother CJ came in.

Brother CJ was a tall white man who owned a New Orleans family-style restaurant called Brother's, and he gave me a part-time job. My shift started at eleven, just before lunch, and I left at two to pick the kids up from school. Then, depending on the day of the week and the number of customers at the restaurant, I sometimes returned for a second shift from four to seven. I didn't mind the work, though I couldn't help but notice there wasn't a single black person at the register. The few of us who worked there were all in the back.

I worked for CJ for six or seven months, and people at church and at home were impressed as they saw me evolve. I had made a serious lifestyle change, was disciplined and focused. My family and friends realized I could handle more, be more, do more, and by that time, I *wanted* more. One of the other entrepreneurs in the church was an attorney who needed help in her office. I jumped at the opportunity. That was how I got into the administrative profession and a regular nine-to-five work schedule.

Working for Eunice, I didn't come home smelling like fryer grease. The front desk was mine; I answered calls, greeted clients, prepared legal documents from templates, and collected money. For the first time, I realized other people made a whole lot more money than I thought I ever could. The smallest check anyone brought in to pay for Eunice's services was five hundred dollars. *Five hundred dollars!* The checks came in every day. This was a lifestyle I knew nothing about. On top of that, Eunice was black. She showed me what a young black woman could achieve, if she worked for it.

The most compelling part of watching the money flow through Eunice's office was seeing how much she gave away. *When you have more money, you can give more.* Any time her family needed help, they called and she wrote them a check. Even though she had recently become a single mother, she was able to help others without worrying about her own bank account. That was powerful.

Because of what I was learning through Eunice, I toyed with the idea of giving college a second chance. I also looked into the military. I thought the army could teach me a lot more discipline and structure, and it was a way to get a free education. After a year of engaging the recruiters, however, they finally told me to come back after I lost twelve pounds. Twelve pounds. I'd lose that in boot camp! *Their loss*, I thought.

Through all of this, I continued to attend youth services at church. Though I was still a teenager, other parents wanted me out of the youth department. I was the only person in the group who had kids and wasn't married, and I sensed they were worried I might be a bad influence. While no one came right out and said, "Maybe you should find something else to do on Fridays," I felt the pressure.

In the three or four hundred families who attended the church, only twelve or so were black. Mother Jessie, who had five sons, continually tried to set me up with her boys. Church folks were always trying to marry off somebody, but I knew it took a lot more than a belief system to make a marriage work. One of her sons, Terry, was an engineer, and Grandma liked him. We dated for a few months and even had preliminary conversations about marriage. If I pointed to something I liked in a store, he wouldn't buy it right then, but I'd be holding it in my hands within a day or two. His goal was to make me happy. But something didn't feel right.

"What's your favorite restaurant?" he asked me one day over the phone.

"Taco Bell." I didn't even have to think about my answer. I was a teenager. What did I know about restaurants?

Terry laughed. He was at least twenty-six and college educated. He thought my response was hilarious. "That's not real Mexican food. I'm going to take you to a real Mexican restaurant."

We hung up, but that whole conversation—and his laughing at me—got under my skin. After church the following Sunday, he made good on his promise. The waiter took our order, and I got the deluxe nachos, which seemed the closest to what I ate at Taco Bell. When I tasted the food, I was shocked. *This is better than Taco Bell?* I didn't say anything at the time, but I didn't finish my plate. That was the beginning of the end of us.

I gathered up all the things he'd bought me from the time we started dating and put them in a box. Later that evening, I called to tell him it was over.

"I left everything you gave me on your mom's front porch." My stomach twisted. Even though he'd hurt my feelings, this wasn't a discussion I wanted to have.

"What?" he said. "What's going on?"

"You should call your mom and have her bring the box inside. I don't want anything to happen to it."

"Toni, why are you doing this?"

I sighed. "We're not moving forward in this relationship. I think you're beyond where I've been and what I've experienced."

"I don't care about that."

"But I do. Terry, it's not going to work."

I hung up the phone. It immediately started to ring. He kept trying over the next few weeks, but I couldn't take his calls. Talking to him hurt. Eventually he reached out to Grandma, and she asked me about the situation.

"Toni, I got a call from Terry. Did you break up with him?"

"Yes. I don't think he is right for me."

"Little girl, you shouldn't be so picky. You are going to pick right up on some stuff. Watch what I tell you."

Whatever, I said to myself. I wasn't about to start letting people tell me what to do.

I started to drift away from my home church to spend time in Pastor Williams' Friday night services. Bruce and Elaine Williams lived two doors down from Grandma and Jesse. Years earlier, they had taken my siblings and me to vacation bible school every summer. When he realized I was serious about God, Pastor Williams started to check in on me. It gave me another place to go, and most of the folks in their circle were black. Little by little, I transitioned from First Pentecostal Westbank to their church.

The doorbell rang one day while I was at their house. A little girl stood on the stoop.

"My mom's having a hat show, and she wants you to come," the girl said to Lady Williams.

Lady Williams smiled as the little girl ran away. Then she said, "I don't want to go to a hat show. I have enough hats, and besides I can make my own! Why don't you go, Toni?"

"Okay." I walked down the street and knocked on the door.

The woman who answered was another pastor's wife, and she gave me a friendly but confused smile. "Good afternoon. How can I help you?"

"I'm here for the hat show."

"The hat show is on Saturday."

"Oh, I'm sorry. We were confused."

"Come on in," she said as she waved me in. "I'll show you what I have since you're here." She kept up a friendly stream of chatter as she showed me the hats and accessories she already had on display.

"Good afternoon, Pastor Clayton," I greeted her husband as we walked past the living room. He sat on the sofa watching TV. His gaze lingered on me for a minute, his eyes thoughtful, and then he went back to his program. I didn't think anything of it, but two days later, their oldest son called out to me while I was walking down the street with Lil John.

"Hey, Sister Toni, come over here."

"What's up, Arthur Jr.?"

He pointed to a skinny man standing with his group of friends. "You should meet Gary. He's on my father's ministerial team." Arthur stepped back as we approached. I wanted to run. By now, I realized guys just used me, and I had no interest in being used. I also had no interest in Gary's matching shirt and socks combination. To me, he looked like a prima donna.

Gary smiled at me. "What's your name?"

"Toni Coleman," I said, uncertain at first. My I-don't-need-you attitude kicked in quickly, and I added, "But that's *Miss* Coleman to you."

He laughed at my sass and shifted his attention to my son. They talked for a few minutes as I watched. I didn't quite know what to make of Gary. He was too skinny for me—he looked as if he hadn't eaten in two weeks—and his skin was much lighter than that of the guys I usually dated. As I tugged Lil John's hand to walk away, Gary stopped me.

"Can I get your phone number?" he asked.

"Sure, whatever," I said.

Gary called and came around often. He didn't seem like such a bad guy, so I couldn't bring myself to be mean to him.

The few times we went out together, he picked places where the kids could go. He took us to fast food restaurants that had playgrounds, and he and I sat and shot the breeze while the kids ate their Happy Meals and ran around the playground. I never let him buy me anything. I thought I had guys figured out; if I didn't let them buy me anything, they couldn't expect anything in return. Our conversations were mostly superficial and centered on church activities. Gary told me grand stories; at one point, he supposedly had three jobs. He was a manager at Color Tile, sold life insurance, and was a volunteer firefighter. As much as he called and came by, three jobs didn't seem possible. My gut told me not to believe him, but I didn't know.

One day, his face took on a serious expression. "God recently showed me a vision of my wife," he told me.

I looked for the kids. I didn't want to get into a deep discussion with him.

"In this vision, we were in my house and she was sitting on the floor in front of me," he continued, "I was combing her long, silky hair and she had your skin color."

I shifted uncomfortably. I fit the vision, but I wasn't sure if he was right for me. "I guess I'm the woman in your vision, huh?" I laughed nervously, thinking *God, you are* not *about to make me marry someone I don't even like.*

"Why do you have to be like that, Toni? Don't you want someone who's responsible and can help you take care of your kids?"

Maybe he had a point. After all, going for guys based on initial attraction hadn't gotten me very far. I shrugged but smiled at him.

I didn't realize how central to my life he was becoming until Lil John ran up to him one day.

"Daddy!" he called, stretching his arms out.

My heart was moved. I wasn't the only one who had become attached to him.

In October, when we'd been dating for four months, he planned a move from New Orleans to South Bend, Indiana. He had better job opportunities there. It was the same reason Big John had moved to Texas, but this was different.

"I want to marry you, Toni," he said over the phone late one night, "but I don't think I can take care of you and the kids with the jobs I have here. I'm going to move to Indiana with my parents, and I'll be back in a few months to get you. When I come back, we'll get married and then you can come up north with me."

I wasn't sure what to say. When I started seeing Gary, I was dating Eddie, who was in the military and had been gone for a year. In the back of my mind, we were still together. I wasn't sure either of them was right for me, but the next time Eddie called, I ended the long-distance relationship. The more I thought about getting married, the more excited I became. Wanting to be married had kept me with Big John long past the time I should've left. Marrying Gary would be taking another step into responsible adulthood—and spare me the embarrassment of answering questions about my children's father.

After Gary moved to South Bend, his parents thought they could talk him out of coming back for me. They didn't want their twenty-five-year-old son marrying a girl with two kids.

"Son, why would you buy a used car when you can buy a new one?" his father asked him.

I was livid when Gary told me. How *dare* his father compare me to a car? I vented my frustration to Grandma.

"I'm a human being, not a car," I almost shouted. "Besides, wouldn't you rather have a used Mercedes versus a new Pinto?"

The friction continued all the way up to the wedding. My family was going to pay for the wedding, and Vivian, who was now my spiritual mother, was funding the reception. Gary's parents only had to pay for the rehearsal dinner. But they never made their deposits for the event. Then, a week before the wedding, Gary called to tell me they couldn't pay for it.

His parents didn't even show up for rehearsal the day before the wedding. I should've known something was up, but I was busy preparing for the big day and had no time to worry about the in-laws.

The day we got married, a groomsman's car broke down on the highway. Gary called the church, and someone went to pick them up. The wedding was supposed to start at three o'clock. The guys finally arrived at three-thirty, but Gary's parents were still not there.

"What do you want to do?" Ms. Ada, Grandma's friend, asked as we waited in her sleek new maroon Jaguar. *Just Married* decorated the back window.

"My family is here, Gary is here, and I'm here," I said. "If his parents chose not to get themselves here on time for one of the biggest days in their son's life, I couldn't care less. If Gary wants to start, let's start; besides, my family is paying the policemen by the hour."

The New Orleans Gospel Temple was packed with more than two hundred people, some of whom—such as Uncle Joe, LindaKay, Mona, Lorraine, Grandma Mary, and the list went on—had come from both Natchez and D'Lo. Jesse and my brothers had all rebelled against wearing tuxes, so I walked down the aisle alone in the beautiful white dress I'd bought from a friend. With all the drama surrounding the day, my walk toward Gary wasn't a happy one. I still had the nagging question of whether he was truly right for me, but I pushed it aside; I was getting married, and that was that.

The service lasted forty-five minutes. With motorcycle sirens going and lights flashing, a bevy of police officers led our motorcade from the ceremony to the reception, just like on *Days of Our Lives* when Bo and Hope got married. As the wedding party pulled away from the church and made a U-turn to cross the Mississippi River Bridge, we passed his parents heading to the church. They were more than an hour late.

Gary and I didn't have a honeymoon; we took the long way from Louisiana to South Bend. We spent a week on the road getting to know each other while the kids stayed with Grandma and Jesse to finish the school year. With each passing state, we left the memories of Mississippi, Louisiana, and the past behind. Our new life was about to begin.

Chapter 8

Get in the Game

To me, South Bend was the perfect place to live. It reminded me of Natchez, with its quiet, small-town feel. After our weeklong, state-by-state trip, Gary and I lived with his parents for six weeks. I rarely saw them. My father-in-law was a welder and spent most of his time on the road, while my mother-in-law worked across the street from the house as a telemarketer for Signature Group; she didn't come home until six or seven in the evening. Gary worked the second shift at Signature Group, and when he wasn't home, I spent most of my time in our room. Though we stayed out of one another's way, living with my in-laws grated on my nerves. I was ready to have a place Gary and I could call our own.

One of the ladies at church heard me talking about finding a new place to live. Her huge, historic home was split into three apartments. She lived in the middle and agreed to rent us the third-floor unit. My kids were still finishing the school year with Grandma and Jesse, but they would join us soon. I had used up a bit of the trust fund money from my father's estate on the wedding, and my dad's social security and VA checks weren't coming in anymore because I was over twenty-one. Although Gary never asked me to help, I could see we were struggling and I started thinking about going back to school and preparing to join the workforce.

One Sunday after church, our struggle became crystal clear. We were at the mall, and I saw a pair of super sharp shoes. They were calling my name.

"Gary, can you give me sixty-five dollars to buy these shoes?" I asked.

"We don't have that kind of money to spare."

I was floored. What did he mean? How could we not have sixty-five dollars for a pair of shoes? Before I knew it, I responded, "I lived better than this with my grandparents."

Gary's countenance fell. I immediately regretted my words, but I meant them.

Within a few months of moving to South Bend, Gary and I drove to Chicago to visit my cousin Mark, one of the Hugheses. Other than Grandma and Jesse, the Hugheses were always an open door for me. Immediately, Mark tried convincing us to move to Chicago, and I could see Gary gave it serious consideration.

"Nothing's really in South Bend," Gary said on the way back home. "Maybe we *should* move. Besides, don't you want to live close to one of your favorite cousins?"

"No, thanks, I'll pass!" I wasn't interested in moving to Chicago. There were too many people in one place for me, and from what I saw on TV, one of the biggest mob families in history lived there.

"I'm serious," Gary continued. "Mark says he can get me a job at Motorola. Life would be better for all of us."

I dismissed the idea. Aside from the financial struggles, life was already good. We had our own place in a sleepy town. What else did he want?

One weekend while visiting his parents, we sat down in the living room after dinner with the extended family—his two sisters and brother-in-law. Our wedding photos had just arrived from Louisiana, and I flipped through them excitedly, reliving each moment in my head. I passed each picture around the room.

"That reminds me," Mr. Carter said. He tapped one of the pictures against his palm.

"Of what?" Gary popped a video in the VCR and came back to sit with me on the sofa.

"Toni's grandmother came over to talk to us at the reception."

I looked up, interested. "Really? What did she say?"

My father-in-law shrugged. "She said if we did anything to hurt one of her grandchildren, she'd come after us."

"And she was serious," my mother-in-law chimed in.

I almost laughed out loud at the thought. "Are you sure it was my grandmother?"

"Yeah, that's her right there, isn't it?" Gary's father passed the photograph back to me. My passive, mild-mannered grandmother looked up at me with a smile, and I felt a sudden rush of love for her. Grandma would always have my back.

"Honestly, I don't know where she got an idea like that," Mrs. Carter said with a sniff.

I bit my tongue. Had they forgotten about comparing me to a used car? As the two of them sat there shaking their heads at Grandma's audacity, I knew I would never be a part of their in-crowd. Gary's brother Derrick had married his first wife a year before our wedding. Mr. Carter always referred to Brenda as his favorite daughter-in-law. It was a constant reminder they didn't think I was good enough for their son.

We'd only been in our new place for a few months when Gary made an announcement.

"We're moving to Chicago."

"Why?" I said. "I told you, I don't want to go to Chicago. It's too dangerous."

"You don't have a choice. We're going." He gave me a matter-of-fact look that said the discussion was over.

You don't have a choice. You don't have a choice. You don't have a choice. Those words kept repeating in my head. I was just starting to come into my own, to realize I wasn't a kid. When I had thoughts and ideas, I wanted him to listen to me. I wasn't sure there would be any of that in our marriage. Was this really right for me?

In late June, we moved in with my cousin Mark's family in Chicago. The kids joined us in July. Mark and his wife owned their own home and drove late model cars but lived a modest lifestyle. Mark was a workaholic. He put in a lot of overtime at Motorola, starting his days at two in the morning and not coming home until four in the afternoon. His wife, DeJohnda, worked part-time in the evenings as a telemarketer.

Right after the move from South Bend to Chicago, I stopped thinking about school. The cost of living in Illinois was much higher than in Indiana. Lil John was in kindergarten for only a few hours a day; I had to work around his schedule. I went back to my previous profession as a pharmacy technician, and Gary went to work at Motorola. Right before Thanksgiving, we moved out of the Hughes' house and into our own apartment.

Soon after, I found another reason to dislike Illinois. The winter weather was terrible. I'd never heard of snow tires or black ice, and it all seemed dangerous to me. Thankfully, our apartment was only half a mile from my tech job at Phar-Mor and across the road from Motorola.

I didn't intend to switch careers. Working in a pharmacy was a good fit for me, but I needed to make more money. Phar-Mor moved at a much faster pace than K&B in Louisiana, but the best opportunities were at Caremark RX. Caremark had a few openings for techs in their mail order center. They called me the same day I applied and scheduled an interview right away. I had three years of technician experience; I should have been a shoo-in to fill prescriptions for them. I didn't have to wait long to hear back from my interview.

"You have the pharmacy experience we're looking for," the HR representative told me over the phone. "But you would be a more attractive candidate if you had prior mail order or assembly line experience to pair with it. We need to be certain you can handle this fast-paced, quota-driven environment. If you can get six months of experience in either area, we'd love to hire you. Call us back when you are ready."

I could do that. Mark had told us a lot about the opportunities at Motorola, so I applied for a position in their factory. The cell phone business was booming, and the factory offered as much overtime as I wanted. My goal was simple: get six months' experience and reapply at Caremark. My aunt Mary, who had lived in Illinois and worked at Motorola during her second marriage, was in town for the week and gave me some pre-interview advice.

"They're going to look at your application, see you have administrative experience, and try to get you to do office work," she said. "Don't do it. You'll get stuck at forty thousand a year, like a girlfriend of mine. When she divorced, she could hardly make it. Go to the factory and get the overtime. After you get your salary where you want it, you can always go to administration."

Sure enough, the first offer Motorola gave me was to work in their human resources department.

"No, thank you," I told the recruiter. "I'd like to go to the factory."

The recruiter looked at me. She was at a loss for words.

"I think it'll be best for me and my kids' schedule," I said smoothly. The factory workers controlled their own paychecks by deciding how much overtime they wanted to work and when.

"But you have all these administrative skills from the law office," the recruiter protested. "We could use your coordination skills to help with our hiring expansion. We can always find ways to grow your career. We are called staffing for a reason."

I wasn't listening. I was going to follow Aunt Mary's advice to the tee. Even though she was a single mother, she always took great care of her kids. She made sure they experienced life and were cultured, while I was making my brothers and sisters mayonnaise sandwiches and bumming food from her house. I wanted to give my kids the kind of life her children had, and I was going to follow her guidance.

Initially, I worked in a manufacturing area soldering parts onto circuit boards to be used later in bay stations or cell towers. The line took up a third of the gigantic warehouse. Each of the six to eight people in my group had to retrieve parts from a staging area for each new circuit board, and then sit around one soldering table assembling them. Sometimes people hogged a bunch of parts so they could work faster and fill their quotas. Once we did our part, the boards moved farther down the line to the technicians for wiring, and then to packing and shipping.

Working in the factory was an interesting experience for a small town girl in the middle of a bunch of big city folks. People traded boyfriends and girlfriends like crazy on the production floor. Every week, I witnessed people fighting over someone else's spouse, changing partners, or getting divorced. Even though men hit on me, I stayed out of it; that was too much drama for me.

After a few months of soldering circuit boards, I moved on to material handling. My new job was to make sure the soldering tables had all the parts they needed to keep production running smoothly. I found ways to cut costs, which opened up more opportunities for me. Motorola rewards employees for creating processes to improve efficiencies, save money, or increase return on investments. One of my first suggestions was to bundle all the parts for each circuit board into one neat little Ziploc bag. I talked the process through with a few colleagues, and they helped refine the idea into a more sophisticated process. Our manager vetted the idea through the formal approvals, and it saved a lot of time for all three shifts. It felt great seeing the idea implemented, and the team and I were monetarily rewarded for our efforts.

My job was ideal, and I loved being at home during the day when my kids got out of school. I also had a team to share work ideas with and managers who helped push me to the next place on my work journey. However, my friend Liz McClain saw things differently.

"Toni, you shouldn't be in this factory," she said to me one day.

"Why not?"

"You don't belong here. You're too smart. Look at the ideas you're coming up with to save money. You should be in administration somewhere."

I laughed it off. "Whatever, Liz. I can make six hundred dollars a week, and my husband can make six hundred dollars a week. Girl, that's enough money. Leave me alone. I'm happy!"

Because I bored quickly, I was always looking for new skills to master, and Liz and another mutual friend, Easter Hill Goodwin, kept encouraging and mentoring me. Every time I went looking for something new, Liz and Easter tried convincing me to apply for a position in administration. I just wasn't interested.

As I finally tired of running from production area to production area at the 1501 building, a position opened in Easter's area, and she wouldn't let me off the hook until I applied. She spoke with her team leader and manager about me joining them, and I landed the job. My focus was on learning large-scale receiving, stocking, and distribution skills, while watching Easter run the administration area of the largest materials location on the campus. Six months after taking the position, Motorola expanded an order to increase cell phone production and opened another material location across the street, the 1475. Easter put in a good word for me, and I was chosen to go to 1475 to help them set up the new location. The basic job requirements were the same, but the administrative portion of running 1475 was all mine. Good thing I had watched Easter. In addition to making sure we were fully stocked, I had to run all the reports and ensure they got to each manager efficiently and effectively. When I ran into system glitches, I called on Easter for help. I was still going to be an hourly employee, but I'd earn a higher wage on the office and technical scale instead of the manufacturing scale. It was a huge growth opportunity for me.

In 1475, the warehouse was still huge, but it was sectioned off into separate departments instead of one big open area. My supervisor, Lester, and I touched base every other week. No need to micromanage; drive, initiative, and task orientation were my signature strengths. We always talked about my work performance and training because the position was new and they wanted an experienced person to run it. But after months at the 1475 location, my new pay still hadn't kicked in. Lester was committed to helping me land the role and had frequent discussions with his manager about it.

One afternoon, Lester came to get me for an unscheduled meeting. He wore a pale, sheepish expression. It was two o'clock in the afternoon when we sat down in the deserted cafeteria to chat.

"Everybody thinks you're doing a really great job, Toni."

"Does this mean the position is finally permanent?" I asked. "What about the new pay?"

"We're going to keep the position . . ." His voice shook, and he trailed off.

I waited for the *but.*

"I'm sorry, Toni. Tim just told me—I cannot hire somebody without a college degree on the office and technical pay scale to do this job. He believes thirty thousand a year is too much for someone without one."

I was shocked to see tears pooling in the corners of his eyes. "So what are you saying?" I asked, though I knew exactly where the conversation was going.

He looked as devastated as I felt. "I got the position

approved, but not the person. You can continue doing the job, but on the manufacturing pay scale."

Though my voice was controlled, I was irritated and insulted. "No worries, Lester. Please find me someone to train because in two weeks, I'm going back to my old department. I will not continue to do a job I'm not being properly paid to do." I got up and started to walk away but stopped to add, "And by the way, make sure Tim knows he already has several of my clear cousins doing similar jobs without degrees." I was, of course, referring to Caucasians.

There was nothing else to say. I had proved I could do the job, but because I didn't have a piece of paper, Tim was not going to allow Lester to hire me. It was all a bunch of hogwash. I went home perplexed and dejected.

After picking my face up off the floor, I determined no one was ever going to tell me again I couldn't have a job because I didn't have a piece of paper. This country girl knew all about games, but—more importantly—I knew in order to get into one, I needed a ticket.

Game on, I thought. *Roosevelt University, here I come!*

Part 3

Knowledge: The Key to Unlocking Destiny

Chapter 9

Don't Complain—Do

I decided to attend Roosevelt University, which was just across the street from our apartment. The first step for non-traditional students returning to school after a break in their education was a four-semester-hour amalgamation seminar designed to share the university's expectations, and to lay the foundation for disciplined study habits. I also took a number of assessment exams for placement in basic courses. If I followed the seminar recommendations and implemented proper discipline, I could survive the rigorous curriculum ahead of me.

My first discussion with my academic advisor, Karen Gersten, was to figure out which classes I would be taking. Karen was nice and spent quite a bit of time helping me understand my options. I knew I wanted to major in human resources, so we planned my program from start to finish. Though my English comprehension and other placement scores were good, I needed to take a remedial math course. Closing this gap was critical to get me to where I wanted to be. I would need to take advanced classes like statistics, finance, and economics, and without a solid mathematical foundation, I would struggle. But, I didn't have to worry about those right away.

Classes started in January of 1996. The kids were nine and ten years old and fairly self-reliant. I worked Monday through Friday, from seven to three-thirty, and went to school from eight to noon on Saturdays. Candes and John were usually eating cereal and watching cartoons as I dove out the door to school. I never was a morning person and usually made it to class just in the nick of time.

I was very nervous about starting college. I'd been out of school for a long time, and high school wasn't exactly a time I looked back on with nostalgia. Those years were filled with negative talk and bad experiences; I didn't know what to expect here. Would it be like junior high or high school, where the teacher handed out materials and you got right to work? I wasn't sure, but the small class size put me at ease, and I received a hundred dollar a week raise at work that very same week. It gave me a boost of confidence as I walked into my first day of class. That's when it dawned on me: *education eradicates poverty*. Why hadn't someone told me this before?

In each class, professors introduced themselves and shared a little about their backgrounds. Then we'd all introduce ourselves to the class. I got to know more people than I ever would have if I hadn't been forced into those interactions. Left to myself, I would've walked in and out of each class without being noticed more than a handful of times. I was still struggling with identity and self-esteem issues—two reasons I let someone talk me out of HR and into a business degree before my first semester was over.

Slowly, Roosevelt awoke the influential spirit in me. Here I had chosen the school specifically because of its Saturday program, but the university's motto, "Dedicated to the enlightenment of the human spirit," sang out to me. The school was founded in a social era where my clear cousins didn't allow too many people of color into universities. One college that stood against the collective was Central YMCA College in Chicago. The college's board consistently pressured its university president for demographic data on the student body. President Edward J. Sparling refused to provide the information because he knew the board would use it to limit the number of blacks, Jews, immigrants, and women who entered the school. To the school's detriment, the board fired him for insubordination. Shortly thereafter, the majority of Central YMCA's College faculty and students left with Sparling to found a new school. In a landslide student and faculty vote, Thomas Jefferson College—which later became Roosevelt University—was born. President Sparling and his team knew it was wrong to refuse to serve a whole group of people who passionately wanted to learn. They didn't simply challenge an unfair system; they crumbled it to its knees.

The school's interminable spirit made me wonder if there was something great buried deep down inside of me. I loved college but dreaded math classes. The fear of failure and the memories of being the "bad girl" always came flooding back when it was time to confront equations. I wasn't dumb—I'd proved that when I tested into AP classes—but all the negative words spoken to and about me over my life were rooted deep in my subconscious. I didn't even think about tackling numbers until I absolutely had to.

After several years of watching me resist math courses, Karen sat me down and jolted me out of my fear zone.

"Let's talk about algebra," she said matter-of-factly.

I opened my mouth, ready to protest for the hundredth time, but she stopped me.

"It's now or never. If you don't take this algebra class, you can't move on to the higher level courses you need to graduate."

She was right, but that didn't make it any easier for me to face the challenge.

"Toni, I've seen the grades you've earned so far. Why are you so afraid of this class? If you get into Algebra 101 this semester, you'll do just fine. Marlene Sacks is the professor; she can teach anyone. She even tutors people with learning disabilities."

I sat with my arms crossed in silent protest before conceding with a sigh. "Fine, Karen. Fine."

Karen smiled at me. "If you have any problems with the class, come back to see me, and we'll get you whatever help you need."

That push gave me the momentum I needed. I knew nothing worth having would come without some sort of struggle. I buckled down and met the challenge head-on. I began studying twenty hours every week and did just fine academically.

Although Motorola was funding my education, the educational assistance policy changed from time to time. When I first started school, I presented a letter to Roosevelt each semester notifying them my employer was paying my tuition. Then, for a small fee, Roosevelt deferred my tuition payment until the end of the semester. For my struggling family this worked well. But our educational reimbursement policy changed before the start of my second year, which meant I had to pay my tuition in full, submit the receipts to our educational assistance team, and wait for payroll to reimburse me. Suddenly, I was under a lot of financial pressure to stay in school. My family lived paycheck to paycheck. I resorted to paying the school by check at three p.m. on a Tuesday and rushing back to our educational assistance team to drop the paperwork off before they closed at four-thirty. This way, if the lady responsible for processing the paper wasn't on vacation, I could have the money in my bank account by Thursday to clear the check I wrote for tuition. On a few occasions, my strategy didn't quite work, but I got as creative as I could. I was determined not to drop out of school. Someway, somehow, I had to finish the program.

In addition to changing the way I thought about myself, the school's philosophy started to influence the way I thought about the world. Determined to give my children the best education possible, I looked for a permanent home in the Schaumburg school district. We could have afforded a nicer house in Elgin, but there was more riding on this decision than my own comfort and pride. There would be time for a nicer house later; I only had one chance at educating my children.

During my second year of school, we purchased our first home in Hanover Park, a village in both Cook and DuPage counties, an hour outside of Chicago. A twenty-dollar late fee from the association changed my fate forever. I started attending the monthly meetings to understand how the association operated. To me, it was crazy to pay a twenty-dollar late fee on a twenty-six-dollar monthly assessment. That was the amount of lunch money my kids needed each week, and the association was not just going to take my hard-earned dollars. My family was already struggling. Then, much to my surprise, I looked beyond my little family and turned my focus toward the community.

One day, a neighbor mentioned the board's plan to take away our rights to rent our homes. They planned to do it without talking to us. The mere mention of this injustice struck a nerve in me, and I was not going to be silent, as I felt they had no right to do that. We had rules, regulations, bylaws, and procedural processes. If we weren't exempt from following them, neither were they. When we purchased the house, we had the right to rent it, and I was not about to let them take anything from us without our consent.

It didn't help that the board was made up of one color and gender—not a single black, Latino, Asian, or woman served on it. All six of them were white men in their late forties and fifties. After I started going door-to-door to rally the community, I received fines for petty infractions: an unnoticeable hole in a window screen, a small dent in the garage door, a light out, or the basketball hoop left in the driveway. I didn't let it deter me from my purpose. I wouldn't let them silence me, no matter how many fines I had to pay. I was going to alert everyone.

During the several weeks it took me to spread the word, the board continued to use their harassing fines against me and a handful of others—most of whom, notably, were people of color. Many of the Polish and Latino families could not read the notices they were receiving; I watched with horror as a Latino family was assessed high fines they didn't understand. The parents let the board have it in Spanish, asking their young son to translate, and it was obvious to me he wasn't relaying the passionate message they were trying to get across. I told the board that families should receive their information in a language they understood.

"They came to *this* country," board members shot back. "They should learn how to speak English."

"That may be true," I said, "but they have a right to know why they're paying high assessments."

My concerns fell on deaf ears, but different rules for different people didn't sit right with me. I was sure this was the same indignation against inequality the president, professors, and students who started Roosevelt must have felt. Surprisingly, I found myself unafraid to challenge their unfair system.

When my neighbors realized I wasn't afraid to stand up to the board, one by one, they stood behind me. Not only was I breaking the spirit of fear in my life, I inspired others to do the same. I organized a picket against the homeowners' association to protest the unfair treatment of people of color. We wanted a new board that would represent the entire community and treat everyone fairly, not just their friends or people who looked like them. Discriminating against people wasn't right.

I contacted the police department to notify them there would be fifty to a hundred of us protesting the next weekend. If we needed a special permit, I wanted to make sure we had it. I also talked to the board to make sure they knew what we planned to do. If I was going to throw stones about unfair treatment, I wasn't going to hide my hand. We even lined up a video camera just in case something happened while we were out there. This was all very different from the little person trying to hide in the corner of the classroom and ran when things weren't going her way.

As I updated Grandma during our weekly calls, she grew afraid for me. I assured her I was being as careful as I could, but I would not allow people to deliberately mistreat others. I put on a calm, composed face, but I was internally frightened. Who on earth was this masked person occupying my body? I hardly recognized her!

Hanover Park is a medium-sized town, and there are only a dozen or so officers on duty at any given time. I had to make sure everyone stayed safe. I faxed the information about the protest to the village manager and the police department, and I plugged the non-emergency number into my mobile phone, just in case something happened while we were picketing. Sure enough, something did.

The board president, Ray, approached our group before we were an hour into the protest.

"You don't have the right to be out here." He waved his arms at us as though he could shoo us away. "You're in violation of association rules."

I gestured to our cameraman and got right into the president's face. "That's a lie. We have every right to be out here, and we're not going to tolerate your foolishness. You and your friends have been mistreating people for way too long, and we are not going to stand for it any longer."

"You can't be out here," he said again. The veins in his forehead bulged.

"Yes, we can. The board doesn't represent the needs of the people of this community."

"Turn that camera off!"

"No!" I shouted back. "We're not leaving until we get a recall election."

We were out there all weekend, both Saturday and Sunday, talking to residents who passed by. Behind the scene, non-protesting residents put additional pressure on the board. They wanted the embarrassment of the picketing over. Finally, Ray and the rest of the board agreed to a hold a recall election—our first victory!

The second came during the election itself. We needed

two thirds of the residents to vote to replace the entire board. All of a sudden, the board pulled a fast one. They decided secret ballots couldn't be cast, and homeowners would have to write their name at the top of their ballot. My team pushed back as we pressed the biased association attorney.

Susan from my team stood up to the board. "We have never had to disclose our voting ballot before. That isn't even required in a presidential election. Mr. Dickler, please explain to the board our rights, or you will hear from our personal attorney in the morning! We have no problem taking any of you to court. We are tired of your abuse."

He complied. After the secret ballots were counted, my team came up thirty votes short. Enough homeowners didn't attend the meeting because the board, in another shifty tactic, only gave us three days' notice about the election. The board played hardball—notifying homeowners late and scheduling the meeting on a school night, five miles away.

The team went home sad but not defeated. Though we'd lost the recall election, we were successful because we'd forced the board to have it, which had never been done before in the community's fifteen-year history. We immediately planned a strategy for the upcoming general election, only three months away.

· · ·

To win the general election, we needed to meet a small quorum. That was much easier than securing a two-thirds' vote, but it wouldn't come with a lack of drama. Although our voting ballots were supposed to be secret, people were afraid if we lost, there would be retaliation at the board's hands. We had to ensure that didn't happen. My team and I got into a heated written exchange with the board and shared every letter with every onsite resident. Shockingly, there were threats on my life, and people stalked my friends, family, and me. Sometimes I cried in my room for days because of the pressure to back off, but I couldn't quit. My team and I pushed forward, and thanks to how vocal and well informed we'd been, we won the general election by a landslide! We came together collaboratively for one cause. As a result, the association's board was no longer one color, and they were unable to enforce rules on some members of the community and not on others. For the first time in my life, I saw firsthand what could be done if one person with courage stood up and challenged an unfair system.

Meanwhile, back at the ranch, Gary was torn about my newfound community leadership. On one hand, he was happy I was involved, but on the other, my new outspokenness caused additional friction in our home. If I didn't have an opinion about something, I was happy to let him have his way, but no longer would I crumble under pressure or do things I didn't want to do just because he said so. My opinion mattered. I had finally found my voice, and I was no longer afraid to use it.

Work and school were going great. Even during difficult times when I walked to school because my car was broken and Gary got off work after me, I didn't let myself get down. Most of the time I snuck down the side streets, from Penny Lane to McConnor Boulevard, so my colleagues wouldn't see me walking. I didn't want them to know I was struggling. From time to time, a few of them offered me a ride to school, but I usually declined unless it was raining or snowing. I didn't want to bother anyone, and frankly, I was embarrassed.

In our work culture at Motorola, titles didn't matter.

Employees and managers alike were free to introduce new ideas or question decisions. But from time to time, I'd run across a few managers who didn't like "discussions." More often than not, you could wait those managers out because people who stifled innovation didn't last long in our organization. An eighty-five year old company doesn't stay in business following the same old routines every day.

When I left manufacturing and materials, I transferred to traffic and logistics. Fred Abbott, the director of materials, wasn't happy about the way the 1475 situation ended for me, so he called one of his friends and asked him to give me an opportunity to work in his group. He agreed but only if Fred would pay my salary for six months; he needed to "try" me out. Fred had no problem putting his money where his faith was. He believed in me.

Eighteen months later, I landed my first internal administration position working for Ken Skurnak. Ken was the head of an engineering group and had recently created a new support position. I found out later he hired me despite my lack of experience because I had the right attitude, and he believed I'd be a good asset for the team. Sometimes a good attitude and the willingness to learn can take you farther than knowledge, skills, and abilities.

While Ken's team rallied around me, a new vice president moved in to lead the organization. Maureen Governs was Ken's new boss, and she decided it would be a good idea to have all the departments' administrators report to her administrator instead of their direct managers. However, the dual reporting structure didn't add anything but more bureaucracy. The rest of us now reported to someone a half step ahead of us, and there would be no room to grow. All of the administrators articulated the same complaints about the new proposal.

"Did you see her new lunch break rules?" I overheard the other ladies asking each other at the copy machine. "We only get a thirty-minute lunch break because she wants us to take two fifteen-minute breaks throughout the day."

"I don't see what the problem is," another one complained. "This is serious micromanagement. As long as we get our work done, it shouldn't matter when we take any of our breaks."

None of us thought the new reporting structure was a good idea, but no one said anything about it outside our small group. I didn't have time to let my energy drain away by sitting around murmuring and complaining. We needed to take this from conversation to action.

"Ladies," I said, "here is what I suggest."

They turned to look at me.

"Why don't we draft a letter to Maureen and ask why these changes are necessary? We can ask her to outline the benefit to the organization. We know it's her. None of our managers agree with this decision."

"That's a good idea."

I shared my thoughts with Stephanie Marcus, a technology director who worked in a beautiful office directly across from my desk. We'd developed a good relationship, and she was always encouraging me. One of few women role models in our organization, she believed in me and told me so all the time. Her words fostered the glimmers of self-esteem she saw inside me.

"You can lead this effort, Toni. If you want me to help you draft a note, or if you want me to look at what you come up with, I'll be happy to do it."

"Thank you," I said, gratified. "I would appreciate that."

"It's no problem. You're good at what you do, and you're right. What they're trying to do doesn't make any sense."

I wrote the letter, Stephanie proofed it, and then I sent it to Maureen. I copied all the administrators and each of their managers, because I wrote it to read as though it were from all of us. The next day, the vice president called all the administrators to her office. It was a beautiful office, with a huge picture window looking out over the city.

Maureen turned to look me squarely in the face with her shrewd eyes. Her short, dark hair swayed. "I know you wrote this." She held the letter in her hand. "Why are you putting up such a fuss about this? What is the problem with my proposal?"

The administrators huddled together near the door of her office. This woman didn't get to where she was by being a pushover. I stepped up to meet her challenge.

"Maureen, we shouldn't be reporting to someone who is technically on our level," I said.

"You all need to cover for each other when others are out. The best way to do that is if all of the admins are on the same team."

"We're already on the same team. All of our managers work directly for you. Or has something changed since we walked into your office? Your admin doesn't have any administrative experience, and she is cocky and arrogant. Some of the other women here have fifteen to twenty years of experience. Personally, we think there is a better solution, and here's what we propose."

Maureen backed off her plan and ended the discussion by telling us to collaborate more. At the end of the day, her only expectation was for us to cover for each other when someone was on vacation. We already did that.

Feeling it was time to move on and find another opportunity to grow, I landed my first executive administration role by transitioning from the engineering team to Global Financial Shared Services. My new role was to support Corporate Vice President Steve Monaco. Once again, I beat out candidates with superb knowledge, skills, abilities, and many years of experience because I had the right attitude.

I loved working for Steve because he cared about his team and made sure we were properly trained and developed. He expected competence and excellence every time I walked into his office.

"Steve, I . . ."

His head slightly turned from his computer to look up at me. His serious face stopped me dead in my tracks.

"Toni, I don't know what you are about to say, but I don't take excuses. If you are about to tell me why you are not going to meet a deadline, I suggest you go back to your desk." He turned back to his computer as if I were already gone.

That discussion, if you can call it one, changed my life forever. I walked the fifty feet back to my desk, pondering his statement. I was working for a kind but extremely focused executive; it was clear I would deliver on time, every time, without excuses. From that day, fourteen years ago, to this one, I have missed three deadlines. Come hell, high water, or coffee-fueled all-nighter, I delivered.

In 2003, after seven years of working, raising my children, and going to school, I finally earned my undergraduate degree. The ceremony was held in Chicago at Roosevelt's Auditorium Theatre. It was a beautiful, historic space—one hundred and twenty years old, restored with gold-leaf ceiling arches, grand murals, and crushed velvet. Over the years, the theatre had seen everyone from Theodore Roosevelt to Jimi Hendrix and Aretha Franklin on its stage. That day, it would be me.

The auditorium was filled to capacity. There were nearly eight hundred students participating in the ceremony. Our families and friends filled the rest of the seats. Gary, Candes, and Lil John were up in the balcony, and many of my colleagues were there. I felt a swelling sense of accomplishment as my name was finally read.

"Toni L. Coleman Carter."

As I walked across the stage, I heard my husband and my girlfriend JoMarie Blissett cheering me on from the balcony. Tears threatened to fall as I walked across the stage. I thought about all the times I walked to school in the cold, rain, or snow, and the times when it seemed as though I wasn't going to complete the program. I remembered the times I tried to keep my tuition checks from bouncing at the school, the occasional conversations I had with Grandma about dropping out because she wanted me to be home and focused on the kids. She reminded me on more than one occasion my time for school had passed; I'd already had my chance and blown it. For once, Grandma was wrong. The last seven years had all led up to this moment. I shook hands with a long line of professors, my dean, and the university president. I had done it.

Even so, before I reached my seat again, my mind was on to the next phase: graduate school started in three weeks. After years of struggling, living from paycheck to paycheck, not knowing how I was going to make it, I'd beaten the odds and earned my ticket to the game. But most importantly, I'd set an example both Candes and John would follow. Changing my destiny automatically changed theirs.

Chapter 10

Life's a Journey, Not a Destination: Never Give Up!

After Steve retired, I stayed in finance for two more years before transitioning to the Human Interaction Research Lab to work for Tom MacTavish, a technology vice president. I nailed the interview with Tom's team, but I was also highly recommended by Michele Johansen, the last administrator to hold the position. Michele loved working for Tom, but his team was expanding and needed to move to a new location. She didn't want to transfer, so she suggested me as her replacement.

"You come highly recommended," Tom said. "I'd like to give you the opportunity to work in this department, but from what you've told me about your goals, I'm afraid as soon as a job opens up for you in HR, you'll leave."

"I'm two years away from finishing grad school," I told him. "I'm pretty sure I won't leave before I finish my degree."

He looked at me for a minute. "'Pretty sure' isn't good enough. If you can give me a two-year commitment, the job is yours."

I took the job. I had learned to be extremely disciplined and focused working for Steve, but working in Tom's organization was a divine assignment in terms of learning how to treat people with the utmost dignity and respect. Although people generally liked me, watching Tom made me realize I was missing something in my interactions.

Tom always shared methodologies introducing human behavioral models. He knew every person on his team and had lunch in the cafeteria with Illinois-based team members three or four times a week. The most important thing I learned from him was to treat people how *they* want to be treated. That is very different from the "treat people how *you* want to be treated" philosophy. It took me a few years to master this fully, but once I did, I turned back to my quest to find a job in HR. It didn't take long to realize I'd missed the organizational politics class in college.

People in HR didn't know who I was, and they were reluctant to take a risk on me. Every time I applied for a junior-level role, the door slammed in my face. I never thought I would have a problem transitioning into HR. My track record was excellent, and I'd knocked every job I had over the years out of the park. You didn't move from manufacturing to where I was by doing mediocre work. On top of that, the company paid for both my undergraduate and graduate degrees. That was a good eighty thousand dollar investment. What a waste to let me sit in executive administration! I realized attitude and performance weren't the only things that mattered—I needed connections.

In the meantime, graduate school was exciting. Instead of memorizing facts and untangling algebra and statistical data, we read case studies, formulated strategies, debated labor relations issues, dissected mergers and acquisitions, and analyzed organizational behavior. It turned out focusing on business as an undergraduate was an excellent move. Had I majored in HR, the way I originally wanted to, I would have needed to get an MBA. Combining functional and business degrees had become a best practice.

My executive leadership class, in particular, shaped my thinking around understanding team dynamics. Dr. Peter Sorenson and Dr. Theresa Yeager co-taught Executive Management 434, which taught us how to create high-performing teams.

"Here's what we're going to do," Dr. Yeager said to us on the first day of class.

We all sat facing the blackboard in the front of the room.

Dr. Sorenson handed out a list of twenty items, while Dr. Yeager finished writing the assignment instructions on the board.

"You're stranded on an island, with only the twenty items on your handout. You have one month to get off this island, or you'll die."

Dr. Yeager turned around, chalk still in hand. "Are there any questions?"

I read the list of items on the paper. *How is this list of junk going to get me off a deserted island?*

Our professors smiled. "Now, get yourselves off the island."

We worked on the assignment individually for twenty minutes. Not a single student managed to get off the island with the list of supplies we were given.

After breaking the news of our deaths, our teachers put us in six teams of four and had us talk through the problem together. At first, I didn't understand what they were trying to do. What was the point of having us fail again? The assignment didn't make any sense to me—until I saw that by working together, my team was able to survive a bit longer before we died, and two of the teams made it off the island.

"Working alone never gets you where you need to go," Dr. Sorenson said.

"Do you see the power of collaborating with others?" Dr. Yeager asked.

That assignment got me thinking. When working alone, my scope was limited. My background and cultural awareness were different from others and vice versa. We all looked at things a little differently. At that moment, I realized it wasn't just some silly assignment in a leadership class. The more I collaborated with others, the better off I, and my projects, would be. This was a big shift in my thought process. The people who had violated me over the years gave me an unrelenting distrust of people in general, but this class started to bring back my faith in the general population. Fred, Steve, and Tom had all been good to me, too. Maybe, just maybe, I could trust others.

During this same time, I allowed a non-family member into my personal life. Evelyn Brown was a little older than I was but had keen emotional intelligence. Despite her small stature—and her gender—she was universally respected in our church for her wisdom, even by the men's group. Somehow, Evelyn always had the right words for any situation. She'd gone through many struggles in her life, but she was an overcomer. She used her experiences to reach out to others who were hurting. Instead of making people feel worse about their situations, challenges, or choices, she extended a lifeline of hope.

Evelyn spent a lot of time getting to know my family, and when Gary and I began to struggle in our relationship, she was there for me. Gary and I consistently argued about something: the kids, my lipstick color, my fingernail polish, the clothes I wore, me wanting to think for myself, or having a baby. Nothing was ever good enough for him. Around the same time, a young man at work was trying to capture my attention by calling and sending messages. I kept telling him I wasn't interested, but questions wiggled into my mind. Was there someone else out there who was a better fit for me? Was there anybody on this planet who would love me for me? Like trying to get off that island by myself, I could only see one side of my problem. Even after praying over it for a week, I was still struggling to do the right thing. I didn't want anyone to experience the awful pain I felt when Big John cheated on me. Eventually I shared bits and pieces of my struggle with Evelyn.

"You're only human," she told me over the phone. "When you start to wrestle with these feelings, give me a call. I'll walk through this with you."

I hesitated to accept her offer.

"I won't share what you've told me with anyone. I promise."

I thanked her and hung up the phone. Was I really considering talking about my personal problems with this woman? I thought about it for a few days. At church the next Sunday, she asked me how I was doing.

"Well," I said, "he's still emailing me. He's really interested, and I—I'm struggling. All this stress is getting to me. I feel so alone. I just want someone to love and support me for who I am. Sister Brown, is that so hard? Or am I asking for too much?"

"Sister Carter, the same God that said 'peace, be still' is the same God that allows the wind to blow. I believe in you, and I know you can get through this test."

I called her again later in the week from the sanctuary of my room and told her everything.

"Just think through what you're doing." Her voice was kind and steady, loving and non-judgmental. "Don't make decisions in the heat of a moment that you'll regret for years to come. You've come so far. Sit down, talk to your husband, and tell him how you feel. He doesn't seem unreasonable to me."

I thought carefully about what she'd said. I imagined how deeply my life would change if I walked down this path. As little as any of us can see into the future, I imagined how I'd feel if I had an affair. I imagined how a divorce would affect my kids. What would they think about me? How would they feel? I imagined how I'd feel as a single mother again. In the end, talking to Evelyn—*trusting* Evelyn—prevented me from going down a path that would've ended badly. Evelyn kept her word; she never told anyone about my situation. I *could* trust people. I just had to be smart about whom to trust.

By this time, I had several friends in HR. The department held "town hall" meetings every month. At the meetings, senior leaders gave overviews of hot topics from the industry and discussed what was happening in the business. I wasn't in HR, so I asked my friends to tell me when and where the meetings were; and then I crashed them. I sat in to learn anything I could.

One day, a different town hall meeting changed my life. During our CEO's quarterly meeting, I had an *aha* moment as I looked over the collected company leaders. As Ed Zander began the Q&A session, I approached the microphone to speak. While waiting my turn, I tried to talk myself out of asking a very important question. After all, who was I to question the CEO of the company? I pushed aside my internal fears. The injustice was overtly obvious and had been for years, but somehow I'd never noticed it before.

"Good morning, Ed. I'm Toni Carter from Human Interaction Research. I've noticed you don't have a single black person on your staff, and I'm not sure how to interpret that," I said. "When people like me look up at your team, we don't see people who look like us. Therefore, we assume we should never aspire to those positions. There are six billion people on this planet. Ed, are you telling me we can't find one black person qualified to sit on the executive floor? Is that what Motorola is saying to me and to all of us?"

A hush fell over the room. I felt the intensity of hundreds of eyes focused on me.

Ed gave me a perplexed look before breaking out into a half smile. "Where's Kay?" he asked, scanning the faces on his team. "Kay and I were just talking about this. She keeps saying, 'it's not about the numbers Ed, it not about numbers.' But this girl has just stood here and calculated the diversity on my team. Unbelievable."

The tension in the room dissipated as Ed smiled directly at me. Murmurs chased through the crowd, but I couldn't hear what was being said.

"Tell you what," Ed said. "Orlando Ashford, a VP from HR is sitting in the front row. Orlando, raise your hand."

I saw Orlando's hand creep up at the front of the room.

"I want you to hold both Orlando and me accountable for changing this situation. Come back and talk to us in one year."

After the meeting, Orlando and I talked about how we

could change the demographic of our executive team and what the next steps should be. During our discussion, I mentioned I was getting my master of science in human resources management in December.

"I've been doing executive administration for the last ten years, but I'd really like to transition into HR," I said. "Do you think I'll have a problem getting a junior level HR role since I don't technically have any formal HR experience?"

"Absolutely not," he said. "What areas are you most interested in?"

"Employee relations and recruiting, but I'm open to exploring opportunities."

"No problem." Orlando scribbled some names on a sheet of paper. "These are three people on my staff in an area you might like. Contact them and tell them I sent you."

I stared at the list in disbelief. Orlando was going to help me make the connections I'd need to land the job I wanted. Was it really that easy? It couldn't be!

When I got back to my desk, I had tons of emails, and my phone was ringing off the hook. "Way to go, Toni. I've wanted to ask that question forever," said one guy. "Toni, aren't you afraid of being fired?" another wrote. "Toni, *girl*, are you crazy? Aren't you afraid of becoming a target?" one of my friends asked. Later that week, I passed Kay walking between buildings.

"Toni, I listened to the replay." Then she gave me a thumbs-up and vanished.

Although Orlando had given me contacts, I didn't call right away. I had six more months left in the two-year commitment I'd given Tom; there was no way I'd break my promise. Sadly, Orlando left the company to work for Coke shortly before I graduated. As life would have it, my connections deteriorated with his departure. I was back to square one. Ultimately, I scrapped my junior-level aspirations to apply for entry-level positions in HR, and they all came back the same—declined. Recruiter? Declined. Employee relations specialist? Declined. Training and development coordinator? Declined. No matter what job it was, I never landed it.

Almost two years after finishing graduate school, nothing changed. The rejections kept coming, and I was starting to feel anxious about my destiny. If I didn't make use of my degree soon, it wouldn't mean anything to anyone other than me. On top of that, I would need to go back to school. I loved learning, but I didn't want to go back again. I'd already spent ten years preparing. It was time for a career change; I was ready for the next big step, but the rejections were taking their toll.

As much as I felt at a standstill at work, I was making strides in the community. I came home one day to find a card from a Hanover Park Trustee stuck in my doorframe. A note scrawled across the back instructed me to call him. I met him for lunch that same day to talk about diversifying the village.

"Toni, I want you to join my campaign slate," he said.

My first response was to pray about it. I was already so busy that if God wanted me to do this, I needed Him to specifically tell me. After spending some time in reflection and prayer, I couldn't ignore the pull to run.

In 2007, I became the first black elected official in the Village of Hanover Park, as well as the entire northwestern suburbs of Chicago. I was also one of the youngest. The local newspapers and TV stations covered the story—Hanover Park had made history by electing me. After everything I'd been through, I could hardly believe it: I'd made history.

The victory was bittersweet, though. Once the excitement of the moment wore off, I realized *all* of my board colleagues were clear cousins. The village employed over two hundred people, and the majority of them were clear cousins as well. When I did find people of color, they were in the very lower ranks of the organization. All of the department heads were monochromatic, and only two were women. This went well beyond helping residents fight biased fines. There was a lot of work to do to make Hanover Park a place where people of all backgrounds could see themselves working at village hall, if they wanted to. We had to make the community a more equitable and inclusive place for everyone, no matter where they came from.

For two years, we made little progress. The first mistake I made was talking about diversity, instead of inclusion. Whenever I mentioned the word *diversity*, you would've thought I was back in high school, cursing people out. It took two years to get a simple Inclusion and Diversity Committee approved. My board colleagues dug their heels deep into the ground. They wanted nothing to do with the project, no matter how I tried to show the value of having an inclusive and diverse workforce.

The same year I was elected, the Village of Streamwood also elected its youngest trustee, Jason. He and his mother owned a manufacturing company in Schaumburg. Since all of the doors at Motorola continued to shut in my face, I asked if his company had an HR manager. The answer was no. I didn't want to leave Motorola, so I asked if I could work part-time for them to gain experience before my degree lost its market relevance. They were happy to help and, more importantly, to work around my schedule. After ironing out the details, I had my first official HR job, as a senior HR generalist. After all those no's, a yes finally came and I didn't have to leave a place I loved to pursue my dream. Persistence and faith, with enough courage to ask for help and think outside the box, paid off.

I gained experience in recruiting, retention, policy writing, and employee relations. In just four short months, a door began to crack open at Motorola.

In December of 2007, the HR department posted an opening in the Office of Inclusion and Diversity. They were hiring a marketplace representative to manage six business councils, three functional councils, three regional councils, and to help evolve the global Inclusion and Diversity strategy. The team went on recruiting trips with the talent acquisition team, represented the company at community events, and collaborated with everyone. The role was everything I loved about HR, but until then I didn't even know it existed.

I started my new job in January and was soon living the dream. Despite what some people may think, diversity efforts don't take opportunities away from a certain group of people and give them to "unqualified" people of color. The position is all about creating high-performing teams, finding the right human capital for the job, leveraging experiences, and maximizing the return on investment for the business. An organization can be diverse without being inclusive, but inclusive organizations are automatically diverse. Diversity is a byproduct of inclusion. The staffing team and I made sure we recruited from all the right places. We looked to the National Association for Asian Professionals, the National

Association for Black Engineers, the Society for Hispanic Engineers, and the Society for Women Engineers—and I loved every minute of it.

In 2009, my political allies created another campaign slate, and this time our entire team won. We were now the board majority and running the ship in Hanover Park. One of the first things the new mayor did was to appoint a deputy mayor. This person would step in and fulfill his duties when he was unable to do so or if he became incapacitated. He chose me—a small town girl who was once depressed, hopeless, suicidal, shamed, unloved, and written off by others. I'd been through hell and back but was now the deputy mayor of a village with forty thousand residents, helping manage its thirty-six million dollar budget. I was president of the homeowners' association, mentoring and coaching others, and growing the career of my dreams. Unbelievable, unimaginable, but completely possible in America.

At the end of the day, we should all live in faith and lead with hope—hope for fairness and justice, dignity and respect, love, and equality. Hope for a future unchained from the past. No matter where we've come from, we can do and be anything we want. Our destinies have no limits, except the ones we place on ourselves. Believe in the impossible and keep pressing through your no's. Even if God has to send someone from halfway around the world to open your door of opportunity, as He did for me with Candi Castleberry Singleton, trust, believe, and know, it can happen. It *will* happen. Changing your life only takes one yes—believe!

Epilogue

Over the years, my energy was reserved for surviving emotional, financial, sexual, and domestic abuse. Surviving the scorn and judgment of being a teen mother. Surviving the limited opportunities that came with a high school diploma. Based on the things I've been through, I should be dead, living in the projects, or in someone's insane asylum. Instead, I'm walking around in my right mind, making effective and necessary contributions to society. I've fought for my family to leave mediocrity behind, and we've set a solid foundation for generations to come. I trained and developed two children who are both college educated, and contributing to the benefit of society. If I don't accomplish anything else in life, I've done enough.

Although I spent years of my life mad at God because of all the bad things that happened to me, I look back now and ask—if all these things *hadn't* happened, who would be yelling loudly from the rooftop, to America and the world, "We are in a global crisis!" I've protected Candes and John from the pain of sexual abuse, and now I'm ready to help others. Children come into this world innocent, and their environments make them who they become. We *must* protect them, because they can't protect themselves.

The circumstances I was dealt as a child were beyond my control, but with a few key people supporting and pushing me to the next dimension, I've achieved more than I ever dreamed. For most of my life, the people who believed in me were my grandma Liza and the Hugheses. They were constant stabilizers in my fraught, unstable, world.

Later in life, I met people like Fred Abbott, a Caucasian male who believed in me and put his credibility and budget on the line for me. He knew I could do more and made sure I had an opportunity to prove it. Dr. Christopher Anne Robinson-Easley, Dr. Marty Martin, Mrs. Pendergrass (my eighth grade teacher), Bishop Vivian Barnes, and Pastor Easter Goodwin have all played important developmental roles in my life. So has Candi Castleberry Singleton, Chief Diversity Officer at the University of Pittsburgh Medical Center. Candi sponsored and gave me an opportunity of a lifetime—the job of my dreams—after twenty rejections. Today, I'm living my dream because of all these people. They are my heroes, because they are people who follow the small glimmer of light inside of others. Now that's *powerfully life changing*—and how I plan to spend the rest of my life: helping others!

Afterword

Cultivating Potential: The Making of a Pioneer
By Dr. Marty Martin

I first met Toni in 2002 while teaching at Roosevelt University. At the time, I was also vice president of human resources and a senior executive for diversity at DePaul University. Toni didn't stand out right away in the classroom. She seemed quiet, perhaps a little aloof. Now, of course, I can see she was evaluating me, looking for any hidden agendas I might have before deciding whether she could trust me. I recall one moment in a class discussion when something suddenly shifted, the wrong button pushed, and Toni's face flashed with an expression I can only call *hard*. This was a woman with a past.

As Toni opened up in class, she first impressed me as a student. She was interested in more than getting an A; she didn't approach her study from the perspective of needing a degree as a means to a better paying job, nor did she overly focus on grades. Toni was diligent, deliberate, and assertive in trying to understand others' points of view without being aggressive. When someone offered a viewpoint that differed from hers, she said, "*Please* tell me more. I want to understand your position." Her body language mirrored her interest: her eye contact was curious as she actively listened, letting the other student know that at that moment, he or she was the only other person on the planet. In short, Toni was fully present and engaged, curious but not judgmental. Even if she didn't change her own viewpoint, she was open to the possibility of learning something different.

Over the years, our relationship transitioned from student-teacher to colleagues. She has invited me to participate in different events at Village of Hanover Park, and I have invited her to sit on DePaul's master of science in human resources and Organizational Diversity Concentration advisory boards. Although we've never talked about certain aspects of our pasts (mine was physically violent), I believe we share a connection at an almost unconscious level because of them. Perhaps Toni has felt it, too.

When I was Toni's instructor, it wasn't my business to ask about her parents or grandparents, her siblings or cousins, or the people who went in and out of her life, leaving scars. I always sensed she didn't have a good childhood, but I knew nothing about the abuse she'd suffered or obstacles she'd overcome. Now that I know, I view her as a pioneer, moving into uncharted territories without the benefit of a parental model or guide. Children do not always follow the path their parents set them on, but at least the road is there for them. Toni was stranded in a forest with no idea of which direction she was headed, and even when she didn't have the money to gas up her chainsaw, she hacked her way through with grace and poise.

Some time ago, Toni alluded to writing this book, not as a definitive "I am," but as an "I'm thinking about . . ." She didn't name it by title or subject matter but told me I would "find it interesting." This strategy of piquing curiosity to tease a reaction is very Toni; by collecting early responses to ideas, she saves herself a lot of time, voice, and energy. But she has to trust the people she uses as sounding boards. Over the years, Toni has identified people she can trust. To some degree, she has created a family—one of which I am privileged to belong.

The things Toni has achieved in her life—her successful career, her stable family—are impressive enough, but what makes her remarkable is she hasn't stopped there. She wants to do something that will benefit others. That's the real power in her story. Many individuals dedicate their lives to healing themselves, but Toni continues to commit herself to healing others. *That* is powerful.

Toni's contributions to society remind me of my work; we are both committed to stopping the violence but in two different areas. Toni's focus is on sexual violence. For me, it is workplace bullying. The two, though, are not completely unrelated.

Like those who are bullied, most children who experience sexual abuse keep it a secret. They feel guilty, ashamed, and frightened and don't know how to express what they are experiencing. Often, they make attempts in their own way to notify loved ones, but people don't always pick up the signals. In general, boys tend to act out. They might be loud in school, refuse to follow rules, act or speak obscenely, or be physically aggressive and engage in sexually inappropriate behaviors. Girls might use obscene language as well, but they tend to be more withdrawn, isolated, and fearful.

When I was a practicing psychologist working in a private practice setting and consulting with law enforcement professionals, I looked for physical gestures and postures that were inappropriate for a child's age as an indicator of sexual abuse. I learned as much as I taught. For example, whether the child is a boy or a girl, parents, grandparents, or guardians should be on the lookout for masturbatory behavior. Children may fondle themselves, other children, or even adults. They may eat in ways suggestive of oral sex. Lastly, children who are victims of sexual abuse may also exhibit changes in sleep or eating behaviors. For some children, night terrors are a big sign something is wrong.

The signs for toddlers and preschool-aged children are often more subtle because the children may lack vocabulary to express what has happened and what they are feeling. If that's the case, watch how they play with dolls and action figures. If the play is of a sexual nature, this may be a sign of sexual abuse. Another avenue is to ask children to draw pictures. Give them a chance to draw anything they wish. Then ask them to draw a house, a tree, a person, or their family; these are standard drawings for assessment purposes. Anything resembling a sexual position or genitals is a possible warning sign. If their drawings are blacked out and/or drawn over and over again, this may indicate anxiety. Please explore it.

Depending on your relationship to the child, there are many resources available for suspected sexual abuse. *For parents*, if your primary care provider is open to discussions regarding mental health and has time to talk to you, go there first. If not, look within your community for a licensed child counselor, clinical psychologist, or a child psychiatrist—someone who specializes in working with children. Let these professionals guide you through the next steps. If you feel the mental health professional minimized the problem, get a referral and a second opinion. Don't allow the lack of health insurance or the lack of money to prevent you from seeking help for your child. Many community-based mental health centers have sliding scale fees based on income, and university-affiliated clinics often offer free services for those who have no income. Again, *income and insurance should not be a barrier to stopping the cycle of abuse.*

For others—educators, coaches, and relatives—please contact a local social service agency. Don't worry about the risk; they will keep your information confidential. If you are right about your suspicions, you will help save a child. If you are wrong, the case will simply be closed. However, I encourage you to let a trained professional handle it.

And remember: *you don't have to be the victim of abuse to be affected by it.* Some people experience abuse vicariously by hearing about it from siblings or friends. It's not as traumatic, but don't underestimate the negative effect it can have on you, especially in generating feelings of guilt. Take care of yourself by seeking a licensed health professional or, perhaps, someone from the religious community. If your family has a history of abuse, even if you have not directly experienced it, family therapy is another option to address how to prevent the cycle from repeating.

Finally, if *you* are the victim of abuse, you must first recognize there was little to nothing you could have done to stop it. But the powerlessness ends there. You have more power and access to power than your abuser would have you believe. This power comes from many sources—loved ones, mental health professionals, law enforcement professionals, religious figures, and even God. The key is not to succumb to the mistaken belief that "time heals all." Time heals mild cuts and bruises. Time heals little arguments with loved ones and colleagues. But, in most cases, time does *not* heal sexual abuse. In fact, not only do you experience the abuse the very first time it happens, but you also re-experience it at various major life stages, such as puberty, first consensual sexual encounter, marriage, pregnancy, childbirth, marriage of children, becoming a grandparent, and on and on. Do not give your abuser the power to taint your entire life. You may not have been able to prevent the sexual abuse that occurred many years ago, but you can prevent re-experiencing the abuse so you can live a richer, more fulfilling life. You are more than your experiences. You do not have to remain a victim.

To start the true healing process, I suggest meeting with a trusted advisor, whether it's a professional, religious figure, or dear friend or family member. Make sure they really understand you. Be certain your advisor encourages you to grow and develop. Challenge yourself to throw off the "victim" label and embrace words aligned with living a rich, enjoyable life. *That* is the life you deserve.

In writing this book, Toni is opening a conversation that will be cathartic to many—but not everyone will welcome it. Toni's story will pierce through a lot of denial. Her family may say she is breaking a taboo by bringing her abuse to light. The African American community may say she is contributing to a negative stereotype. Or the response may be apathetic; there are hundreds of stories of sexual abuse in books, television, and on the Internet, so why does hers matter? It matters because, like anyone who braves judgment to reveal truth, Toni is displaying true courage in telling her story. It matters because this book is only the beginning. It is the catalyst for a movement, a platform from which Toni can connect with other victims of abuse, connect them to each other, build a powerful network of survivors and advocates . . . and maybe even stop the cycle of violence altogether.

—Dr. Marty Martin

Dr. Marty Martin is currently director and associate professor in DePaul's Health Sector Management MBA program. He is a licensed clinical psychologist and has worked in the health care and human resources profession for more than 20 years. He is one of few psychologists in the country who has dedicated his expertise to stopping workplace bullying in corporate and health care settings. Dr. Martin is the author of *The Inner World of Money: Taking Control of Financial Decisions in 2012;* his second book, *Taming Disruptive Behavior,* will be published in 2013. Please visit his website at *www.drmartymartin.com.*

Part 4

Resources for Self-Empowerment

Lessons Learned

Writing *When Trouble Finds You* was cathartic. It allowed me to reflect upon the many things I've learned over the years as a result of meeting various challenges in my life without being intimidated by them. In this section, I've decided to share what I believe are the five most important lessons I learned. My hope is they'll provide a different perspective and additional insight to strengthen and empower others to overcome their fears—ultimately giving everyone who needs it a swift push to start or continue the healing process!

1 – Children Need Love

Being a teen parent was tough. I now realize I was seeking someone and something to love. I believe that becomes the goal of most teen girls, especially those for whom there's no father in the home. However, if parents meet their sons' and daughters' need for an emotional connection, giving them a sense of belonging and unconditional love *at home,* that is the first step in equipping them with the skills necessary to resist making bad decisions later. By devoting this time and effort, we aid our children in developing a healthy expectation for what love is. And that becomes elemental in reducing their chances for being sexually active at an early age, as well as incidences of teen pregnancy.

Parents:

While preventing teens from becoming parents is a communal obligation, the work begins in our homes. Every one of us must commit to instructing and training our children to resist engaging in adult behaviors in their adolescent years. Consider spending quality time with your children, doing what *they* like to do. It affords us the opportunity to build their self-esteem and to teach them the difference between good and bad relationships. Having developed this awareness under our guidance, when their inevitable moments of choice arise, they'll be better equipped to resist peer pressure. And the research shows . . . we are their primary source of influence. There is hope!

Teens:

Let truth be your guide. I encourage you to be honest and share with your parents what is in your heart. As antiquated as they may seem, your mom and dad have been where you are now, and they want to do what is right for you. Since no one person knows it all, if you believe your parents are not fully understanding you, respectfully tell them so. But don't let your discussions descend into bickering, since progress is not made in such a place. If you want them to understand your position, be ready to truthfully explain what you need, mean, and intend. If you are not truthful, no one can effectively help you. Even if you eventually get what you want by deception, you'll undermine your relationship with your parents and damage the trust they have in you—a bad combination whose effects can take years to repair!

2 – Unhealthy Relationships Prevent Growth

It's best to leave an abusive relationship the minute it becomes one. The longer we stay in it, the harder it becomes to leave. Although leaving is not impossible, research shows when people attempt to leave a physically abusive relationship, their lives are in the most danger. If you are leaving an abusive relationship, make sure you have a plan, a safe place to go, and the right support system.

Parents:

For the most part, we are products of our environments and learn from the people who care for us. Always remember: in every relationship, we model for our children what they will consider "healthy" and "normal." From us, our children learn how to treat their partner and what they should tolerate from that person, so we must endeavor to model only good relationship behaviors.

As a parent, I've experienced unhealthy relationships. As you've learned from the book, I entered my first one at a very early age and had little regard or awareness of how to break free. If your child becomes involved in an unhealthy relationship, please be careful with your approach and seek help from a professional. It could be a long journey to freedom for them. It has been for me.

Teens:

Your partner should never put his or her hand on you in an abusive way. The first time someone hits you, leave the relationship. The abuser may cry, plead, or beg, promising to change and that they'll never hit you again. But if you stay, it only leaves the abuser with a sense of justification, and therefore the abuse continues and usually worsens—while for you, leaving only becomes harder. I've never seen an abuser hit someone once and fail to repeat the behavior. I would hate for you to spend years in an abusive relationship. Love yourself more!

3 – Ignoring Warning Signs Spells TROUBLE!

Sometimes relationships change while we're in them. But in hindsight, it's obvious to me I totally ignored warning signs or made excuses for my partners' behavior. For example, when I was pressured into sex for the first time, it shouldn't have taken me by surprise; every phone conversation with the person had some form of sexual content in it.

Parents:

Trust your children, but monitor the people they are befriending.

Teens:

I wasn't ready to be a mother at fifteen. I caused unnecessary hardship on Candes and John by having them early. In their foundational years, they sometimes didn't have the things they *needed* because I didn't have the money to buy them. To prevent this from happening to your kids, I encourage you to wait until you are married, have finished college or trade school, and have completed two years in the workforce. Life will be so much easier for you—and them—if you do so.

How an Abusive/Controlling Relationship Looks and Feels

I stayed in two abusive relationships because I didn't know what a healthy relationship looked like. I assumed my relationships were normal and everybody went through similar things because I consistently saw my mother hit by different men in her life. She dated one married man for fourteen years, and he beat on her—and my siblings and me—frequently. While my granddad never hit my grandma, he was an alcoholic until he was sixty-five years old. He spent money on DUIs that could have been used for other purposes. That relationship was not exactly healthy, either.

By answering the following questions, you should be able to identify whether you are in an abusive relationship. Please answer the questions honestly; you don't have to show them to anyone.

Does your partner:
- Embarrass you, put you down, or make fun of you in front of others?
- Use intimidation or threats to make you comply with requests?
- Threaten to leave you if you don't do exactly what he (or she) tells you?
- Imply you don't love him (or her) if you don't do exactly what he (or she) says?
- Always call, text, or email you, trying to track your every movement?
- Prevent you from doing things you would like to do, such as spending time with your family and friends?
- Prevent you from leaving a place you don't want to be?
- Leave you somewhere to "teach you a lesson?"
- Try to control whom your friends are, whom you talk to, or with whom you spend time?
- Tell you what type of clothes and/or makeup to wear—and not wear?

- Minimize or belittle you or your accomplishments?
- Try to make you believe you are nothing without him (or her)?
- Treat you like a piece of property?
- Blame you for how he (or she) feels or acts?
- Push, grab, pinch, shove, or hit you?
- Use drugs or alcohol as an excuse for abusing you or saying hurtful things to you?
- Pressure you to do things you don't want to do (i.e., have sex, borrow money, etc.)?

Do you:
- Feel afraid of how your partner will react at times?
- Make excuses to other people for your partner's behavior?
- Cover up or hide bruises after you've been hit?
- Feel like nothing you do is good enough for your partner?
- Think your partner has double standards—one standard for you and one for himself (or herself)?
- Believe if you change something about yourself, your partner will change?
- Always do what your partner wants to minimize conflict, although it may not be good for you?
- Stay in the relationship because your partner threatens to commit suicide or kill you if you try to leave?

If you answered *yes* or *I don't know* to even one of these questions, you are probably in an abusive relationship. Please consider talking with a professional to develop a plan or visiting *www.wtfu2.org* for suggestions on how to address this issue. Proper planning is key to staying safe in these situations!

Never underestimate what an abuser will or will not do. Trust me—you never know.

4 – Healthy Relationships are Supportive, Loving, and Fulfilling

In healthy relationships, partners never belittle, shame, or emotionally, financially, or sexually abuse each other. The relationships are whole and complete within themselves.

In healthy relationships, partners are able to:

- Manage conflicts and differences without using intimidation and/or threats.
- Make the relationship a priority by caring for, protecting, and nurturing it.
- Take care of themselves without trying to control the other person.
- Ensure the other person feels special, loved, needed, and wanted.
- Communicate wants, needs, and emotions without shame or guilt.
- Willingly and lovingly attend to the needs of the other person without being forced.
- Keep agreements and be honest with each other.
- Maintain respectful boundaries—no one forces his or her position on the other person.
- Be themselves . . . all the time!

5 – Where My Place Is

People are always trying to define us. Whether at school, work, home, or church, some people always "know better" than you where you should be and what you should be doing.

I've decided my place is where God and I make it. God knows what he created me (and you) to do. *"For I know the thoughts and plans that I have for you,' says the Lord, 'thoughts and plans for welfare and peace and not for evil, to give you an expected end'"* (Jeremiah 29:11)!

I will not allow other people to define or put limits on me—and neither should you. If God, the Creator of the Universe, gave you the knowledge, skills, and ability to do something, do it. Sometimes people try to keep you in a certain place because they have underlying motives that have very little to do with you—but don't allow anyone to stand in the way of your growth, progress, and happiness.

I encourage you to maximize every ounce of potential inside you. If you "fail"—and learn—it really wasn't a failure. My Grandma Liza used to tell me, "Sometimes the best sense is bought sense." I must admit—she was right!

Discussion Guide

The first and hardest step in the healing process is talking to another person about one's experiences. It was no different with me. As contradictory as it seems, there were moments when loneliness and isolation were my only refuge. They formed the walls of my sanctuary, comforting me in the belief and assurance no one else would understand or relate to situations like mine. So bitter silence was my outward response—a silence where the rule of the day called for me to suppress all that was painful.

Over the years, I've learned there's usually at least one person who, if given the chance, would listen to and truly *hear* my pain. Instead of abandoning me, that person would have comforted and consoled me. Where I perceived there was no solution, he or she would have offered guidance on how to move forward. This person would have been my stalwart in the storm. In troubled times, no one is an island, and we don't have to walk alone. In order for our hearts to heal, we have to open up and share our pain and our fears. This can be difficult to do, but in order to heal, we must press through our fears and on to freedom.

To aid in this first step—that is, to break the silence—the discussion guide moves from group analysis and dialogue to personal introspection. In the group dialogue, which is our first phase, we open discussion with a general overview of the chapter's main themes. The purpose is to allow everyone to become comfortable with discussing sensitive and painful topics.

Our next phase is to broaden our discourse of the chapter's themes by exploring how they influenced my growth, whether positively or negatively. This allows everyone the opportunity to explore how they might approach and resolve these or similar circumstances. The goal is to establish a sense of trust among participants of the discussion group. By creating an environment that allows partakers to identify either with the abused or abuser, each person is able to make an easier transition into third part of the discussion guide.

In the latter phase, the goal is verbalized self-reflection. In the safe environment created by the earlier phases, everyone has the space to explore their life and share personal stories without fear of judgment or ridicule. Whether those stories involve experiencing or inflicting abuse, the object is for everyone to share, not to seek resolution or closure . . . just share.

• • •

Just as there are three phases of discourse within the guide, there are three discussion sections within each chapter to facilitate the conversation.

Phase One: Recalling the Chapter

This section opens the dialogue by highlighting the chapter's overall theme(s). Here, everyone discusses the central topic(s) in a general manner. The goal is to explore experiences or share knowledge, as well as listen to the experiences of others. Everyone copes differently with specific problems, with varying levels of tolerance and patience; therefore, we'll likely see a variety of perspectives. It's very important for everyone to take the opportunity to share what resonated with them and listen respectfully to what resonated with others. It's this resonance that opens the "door" into the world of the main character(s) in the chapter.

However, it's important that no member of the group feels forced into making personal reflections known. The main goal is for everyone to create "their door," the entrance point for new understandings and revelations, while keeping in mind we're all at a different stage on our journey.

Phase Two: Responding to the Content

In this section, we cross the threshold of our "door." Here, we seek to delve deeper into elements of theme and character within the chapter. We facilitate this by giving attention to two or three quotes from the text, though the intent is not to limit the discussion. The objective is to spark substantive dialogue. Everyone should have the opportunity to explore how they might feel or react to a given the situation.

Phase Three: Reflecting Collectively

Here, in the final phase, our objective is self-reflection. However, the purpose isn't for us to resolve our problems or seek closure. Simply being able to see how we've endured and overcome offers us the chance to evaluate the challenges and circumstances in our lives. Having earlier visualized—and thereby given some form to—what was once dark, nebulous, and foreboding allows us the opportunity to understand our situation and embrace power to move positively forward.

To facilitate this, I've posed questions centered on the

chapters' themes and requested everyone look into their own lives for answers. I'm hoping we'll affirm: it's not the circumstance or tragedy that defines us; it is our response to it. How we choose to move forward determines whether we are victims or victorious. This is a place where we can take our lives back.

Suggestions for Group Setting

Given the sensitivity of the subject matter, it's necessary to create a community of trust. When we're open and honest, our discussions usually flow better, though taking such steps appears to make us vulnerable. However, we're only vulnerable when we intentionally try to deceive or manipulate others. Nevertheless, we must create environments of openness, dialogue, and mutual respect in order for lasting change to happen.

The Setting

Our purpose is to create a relaxed but contemplative environment. Sitting in a circle allows everyone to feel they have everyone else's undivided attention, emphasizing the sense of importance in what they are saying. Providing refreshments also helps create a sense of community and tends to break the tension among people.

Leading the Group

So no one feels there's a hierarchy of authority, it's best to allow different people to lead the group. First, allow members to choose whether they wish to lead. As time passes, the most reluctant people may become comfortable. Sharing leadership encourages mutual respect and alleviates potentially competitive tensions, which are disruptive and detrimental to the group.

Suggested: Opening and Closing

It's important to begin with prayer or meditation. But given we live in a pluralistic society, this may not be constructive in every situation. Yet allowing a moment of silence, either at the beginning, end, or both, strives to place the group on the same spiritual level while developing cohesion and harmony among the group.

. . .

My desire in providing this guide is to give others what I never had: a tool to help understand the struggles, pains, and sufferings of our past. However you choose to use this guide, my hope is it will become a vital asset in the healing process. I hope we all become better mothers, fathers, sisters, brothers, grandparents, aunts, uncles, and individuals. I also hope we all become more aware of the people we allow into our lives. Doing so will help protect our children and our communities. Although there are many resources available to help people change their lives, I hope, at minimum, that this discussion guide starts the conversation toward healing our hearts, our souls, and our children.

Chapter One
Life and Its Surprises

Recalling the Chapter
What resonated with you from this chapter?

Responding to the Content
- Can you recall a personal story or experience relating to this chapter's themes?
- Did you lose a parent at an early age? If not, can you imagine what it feels like?
- What do you suppose are the effects upon a child whose family continually moves from place to place?

Reflecting Collectively
Discuss one or more of the following, as time permits:
1. How do you believe losing a parent at a young age affects a child's perspective on the world?
2. Is it possible for kids of divorce or separation to experience similar feelings or struggles as those who lose a parent?
3. How can we minimize the negative consequences of losing someone important to our children at a young age?
4. What do you suppose are the effects upon a child whose parent's funeral is held on their birthday?
5. What are some signs of depression we can look for in children?

Chapter Two

Be Careful Who You Trust

Recalling the Chapter
What resonated with you from this chapter?

Responding to the Content
- Can you recall a personal story or experience relating to this chapter's themes?
- Have you ever been left with someone who hurt you or someone in your family?
- How did or does it feel to struggle to provide a safe environment for your children, and yet—despite your best intentions and efforts—the results are unexpected and sometimes detrimental?

Reflecting Collectively
Discuss one or more of the following, as time permits:
1. What precautions can we take when choosing whom to leave our kids with in our absence?
2. What types of behaviors identify children who have been abused?
3. How can we make kids feel comfortable telling us what's going on with them? Keep in mind people who hurt children often use threats of additional harm to silence them.

Chapter Three
Things Are Not Always What They Seem

Recalling the Chapter
What resonated with you from this chapter?

Responding to the Content
- Can you recall a personal story or experience relating to this chapter's themes?
- What do you suppose it feels like to be violated by someone you trusted (relative, family friend, etc.) or held in high regard (teacher, doctor, etc.)?
- How can you free yourself of the bad things that have happened to you?

Reflecting Collectively
Discuss one or more of the following, as time permits:
1. What steps should we take when our kids express discomfort with adults in their lives?
2. What signs of discomfort might a child exhibit when in the presence of an abusive adult?
3. Should we force our kids to kiss their close relatives, such as aunts, uncles, and grandparents?
4. How might we help our kids explain when someone's behavior, toward either them or their siblings, crosses the line?
5. What organizations or services exist to assist us with vetting nannies, childcare centers, or daycare providers?
6. How should we manage instances when our kids become distraught over efforts to leave them at daycare or for their first day of school (i.e., separation anxiety)?

Chapter Four

What Goes Around Comes Around

Recalling the Chapter
What resonated with you from this chapter?

Responding to the Content
- Can you recall a personal story or experience relating to this chapter's themes?
- Have you ever experienced the betrayal of a friend?
- Have you ever been part of a relationship characterized by continuous bickering?

Reflecting Collectively
Discuss one or more of the following, as time permits:
1. How do people behave when they are hurting?
2. What's the impact on relationships of people who have yet to resolve their inner pain?
3. How should we explain death to kids?
4. How do you feel about Toni lying to her grandmother about the fight?
5. Should her grandmother have been so willing to accept Toni's version of the incident?
6. Do you know parents who ignore signs their kids are heading down the wrong path?
7. How do you perceive a parent's failure to notice the decline of his or her child? Is it a lack of attention, indifference, or unwillingness to see something is wrong?
8. What steps do you believe parents can take to bring an end to their child's descent into trouble?

Chapter Five
Some Things Never Change

Recalling the Chapter
What resonated with you from this chapter?

Responding to the Content
- Can you recall a personal story or experience relating to this chapter's themes?
- Have you ever desired the affection and attention of someone who either ignores your advances or doesn't take the time to learn how to love you?
- Have you ever experienced an unceasing sibling rivalry?
- Are you and your siblings struggling with your family relationships?

Reflecting Collectively
Discuss one or more of the following, as time permits:

Talking with our Children
1. How can parents ensure they are building loving and respectful relationships with their kids?
2. What must we do to ensure our kids get the love and nurturing they need to be whole and emotionally stable young people?
3. Why is creating a safe, structured, loving, and disciplined environment for children important for their future development?

4. How might you address your parents concerning the circumstances of your past without making them feel guilty or defensive?

5. How might you receive what your children express to you about their worries and emotions without seeming or becoming defensive?

6. How can we build a healthy sense of self-esteem in our children?

7. How does a healthy sense of self-worth aid in keeping us from looking for love in the wrong places?

Sex and Teens

1. How does a healthy self-esteem aid young people in abstaining from premature sex?

2. What can parents tell their kids about sex?

3. How can we help our kids understand the impact teen pregnancy has on their futures?

Relationships

1. What do you suppose are the root causes of sibling rivalry?

2. What effects can sibling rivalry have on family unity?

3. How might parents prevent or put an end to sibling hostility?

Chapter Six
It's Time for a Change

Recalling the Chapter
What resonated with you from this chapter?

Responding to the Content
- Can you recall a personal story or experience relating to this chapter's themes?
- How do you define an unhealthy relationship?
- How do you appraise a healthy relationship?

Reflecting Collectively
Consider the following, as time permits:

The Idea of Love
1. What is love?
2. How do you know you are loved?
3. What are the differences between love and lust?
4. Is it possible to have a healthy relationship based on lust?

Choosing a Partner
1. Should you seek the approval of family before choosing a mate?
2. What should you do if your family expresses negative impressions or information about your partner?

Domestic Violence

1. Why do people choose to stay in unhealthy relationships?
2. How can you help those trapped in unhealthy relationships understand the negative effects of those relationships?
3. How does self-worth factor in such relationships?
4. When is the best time to leave an abusive relationship?
5. Since domestic violence is a learned behavior, is it possible to unlearn such behavior?

Chapter Seven
The Past Does Not Define Us

Recalling the Chapter
What resonated with you from this chapter?

Responding to the Content
- Can you recall a personal story or experience relating to this chapter's themes?
- Can you recall moments when you faced difficulty changing your behavior in hopes of improving your life?
- What role does family environment have in shaping the way we think and behave?
- How does family environment influence our beliefs as to what is and is not acceptable in relationships?

Reflecting Collectively
Discuss one or more of the following, as time permits:

Life Changes
1. How do you define a life change?
2. Is every change in life a choice?
3. Why is it proper to weigh every choice and decision when creating an action plan?
4. Given there will be pitfalls, failings, and hardships, how do we measure whether we are moving in the desired direction?
5. How might you break free from elements of the past impeding your ability to move forward?
6. How do you manage any relationship that resists or discourages your desire for personal change and improvement?

Marriage

1. What's your definition of "the *right* person" for you?
2. Are healthy marriages always full of drama and difficulties?
3. Should couples receive formal counseling before marriage?
4. When a person is considering marriage, what's more important: age, level of responsibility, or maturity? Or do none of these things matter? What leads you to this conclusion?

Chapter Eight
Get in the Game

Recalling the Chapter
What resonated with you from this chapter?

Responding to the Content
- Can you recall a personal story or experience relating to this chapter's themes?
- How might we stress the importance of a good education?
- What does it mean to "network," and why is it important?
- Why is it important for us to be authentic in a seemingly inauthentic world?

Reflecting Collectively
Discuss one or more of the following, as time permits:

Life Preparedness: Our Kids
1. How can we, as parents, help our kids plan for the future?
2. Is it appropriate for us to direct our children in finding their way, or should we allow them to find it on their own?
3. Are there any tools we should recommend to help our children find focus and clarity about life or a career passion?

Life Preparedness: As Adults
1. Should everyone have a career map?
2. Should we be flexible in pursuing a career, or should we set our sights firmly on a specific role and work toward it?
3. How can we prepare for educational and/or career setbacks?

4. How important is business acumen to everyday life?
5. What is *emotional intelligence,* and how might we develop ours?

Chapter Nine

Don't Complain—Do

Recalling the Chapter

What resonated with you from this chapter?

Responding to the Content

- Can you recall a personal story or experience relating to this chapter's themes?
- Have you ever said or done something that resolved a negative situation?
- Do you believe complaining impacts your health? If so, how?

Reflecting Collectively

Racial separation was declared constitutional by the Supreme Court in 1896 (*Plessy*). More than forty years later, in 1939 and 1947, husband and wife psychologists Kenneth Bancroft Clark and Mamie Phipps Clark performed what is referred to as the "Clark Doll Experiment." In the experiment, Kenneth and Mamie sought to evidence the effects of "separate but equal" on children between the ages of six and nine who attended segregated schools. The psychologists gave each child a white doll and a black doll, otherwise identical, and found black children had a greater affinity for the white doll than the black doll. That is, the children in the study rejected the very doll that looked like them. It's the Clark study that the plaintiffs in *Brown* (1954) used to sway the justices as to the deleterious effects of segregated schools upon black children. So moved, the justices declared policies of racial segregation unconstitutional, overturning the *Plessy* decision. Yet, nearly sixty years later, it appears we've progressed little in the perceptions of "black is bad" and "white is good."

Discuss one or more of the following, as time permits:

1. What can we do to overcome our own unconscious biases so we make more prudent decisions, regarding people who don't look like us?
2. Why might it be difficult for people to accept the concept of being inclusive of all groups?
3. Why is it uncomfortable to deal with people who do not look like us?
4. Does Hollywood's portrayal of certain communities influence what we think about others or how we feel about ourselves in relation to those "others?"
5. How can we learn to appreciate people who have persevered through hard times, regardless of their race but also as a matter of race?
6. Is it fair to compare the successes of those who succeed *despite* the backdrop of social and economic hardships with those who have not experienced such disadvantages?
7. How does education serve as the key to eradicating poverty?
8. Why is it important to share our struggles to persevere against prevailing odds and circumstances with our children?
9. How does your attitude affect your future?
10. Should we be cognizant of our words? Are they powerful?
11. Have you noticed correlations between fear and violence? If so, what are they?
12. How might we begin to resolve our fears?

Chapter Ten

Life's a Journey, Not a Destination: Never Give Up!

Recalling the Chapter

What resonated with you from this chapter?

Responding to the Content

- Can you recall a personal story or experience relating to this chapter's themes?
- Can believing in someone help a person turn his or her life around?
- Is there a pivotal figure in your life whose belief in you became central to you believing in yourself?

Reflecting Collectively

Discuss one or more of the following, as time permits:

1. Would you or have you helped someone you don't know?
2. Do you know other people who have aided people they did not know?
3. Why is perseverance more beneficial than accepting rejection?
4. Do you consider asking for help a sign of humility and strength? Why or why not?
5. What makes having a victim's mentality dangerous?
6. Does feeling like a victim impede future success?
7. Is humility a predicate to our sense of success or being successful?
8. Why is it necessary to cherish the small victories and to teach our children to do so?

About the Author

Toni L. Coleman Carter is the energetic culture, inclusion, and diversity (CID) subject matter expert and HR consultant for a global, $12.5 billion dollar technology organization. She is a change champion who collaborates with business  leaders to create an environment to empower and engage others in order to achieve global competitive advantage. Carter partners as a consultant to create, develop, and manage the CID initiatives, while increasing inclusion awareness and providing governance for the business councils. She has worked in corporate America for 20 years and is the former deputy mayor for the Village of Hanover Park. Prior to joining the High Tech Organization, Carter was in the pharmaceutical and food service industries. She worked for K&B (Katz and Besthoff, now Rite-Aid) and Phar-Mor Pharmacies as a pharmacy technician and as a manager for McDonald's and Taco Bell Corporations.

In April of 2007, Carter was elected as Hanover Park's first black council member. Carter's position at the village allowed her to assist with the recruitment, selection, and appointment of department heads and to help create policy operation strategies. During this time, Carter founded the village's Cultural Inclusion and Diversity committee, the largest volunteer committee in the village. After two years of confronting challenging opportunities, she became the village's first black deputy mayor.

In her position, Carter created a homeless prevention task force that focused on providing solutions to reduce the impact of the 2008–2010 economic crisis, preventing home foreclosures and providing transitional housing for residents. In 2008, she was appointed to Hanover Park's Crime Prevention Task Force, a team that helped design crime prevention strategies and methodologies for the village. The same year, Hanover Park named her Inclusion and Diversity Champion, and she received an Outstanding Leadership Award from Motorola's Women's Business Council.

In 2013, the Illinois Commission on Diversity and Human Relations honored Carter with the Dr. King Workforce Inclusiveness and Community Activism award. The 2010 issue of *Who's Who in Black Chicago* named her one of the most influential blacks in government. She is a member of DePaul University's human resources advisory board, the National Society for Human Resource Management (SHRM), the Illinois Fox Valley SHRM Chapter, and the Delta Mu Delta International Honor Society in Business. She is a certified diversity practitioner and is currently pursuing certification as a senior professional in HR. She holds a bachelor and a master of science degree from Roosevelt University in Chicago.

Carter dedicates part of her life to helping people who have been abused. Her memoir, *When Trouble Finds You*, is a tool of hope, inspiration, and education for others who may have suffered the way she did as a child.

When Carter is not spending time with her family, she loves building community relationships and leveraging strategic partnerships, and teaching at Columbia College in Elgin, Illinois. Her husband, Gary, spends his time training community leaders, and they reside in Hanover Park with three wonderful children, Candes, John, and Taylor.

Acknowledgments

I would like to thank *everyone* who has purchased or read this book. It's people like you who can *help me change the world.* Thank you for supporting this cause. I appreciate each of you.

I am thankful for the lives of the late Jesse and Eliza Taylor, my grandparents. They've inspired me to be all I can be, and supported me even when what they wanted for me conflicted with what I wanted for myself.

To my faithful, covenant-keeping husband, Pastor Gary Carter Jr., and my awesome children, Candes, John, and Taylor: thank you for being a part of my ever-changing and adventurous life. I love you all and appreciate your support. The best is yet to come!

To my brothers, Tracy, Stacy, and Robert; and my sisters, Erica, Ladonna, and Sharon: thank you for making life interesting. Although our lives have had unique and stressful challenges, we've persevered because we're overcomers.

Mom, thank you for giving me life. I pray you find total healing for your hurting heart. Always remember, it's never too late to change.

Thank you to my special cousins: Chanell, Kisa, Eric, Nina, Robin, and the Hughes clan: Mark, LindaKay, Lorraine, and Mona. When everyone else gave up on me, you always believed in me. I decree nothing but the best for all of you.

To my extraordinary friends, JoMarie Blissett, Ken Britter,

author Evelyn Lewis Brown, Pastor Easter Goodwin, Co-Pastor Olieth Lightbourne, Liz McClain, and Evangelist Joyace Ussin—thank you for being my friends, encouragers, and supporters for two decades. That's a long time to put up with such a complex person. You've helped me in more ways than you know.

Bishop Vivian Fleming Barnes, there are no words to express my feelings for you. God used you to change my life forever. Thank you!

Judge Patricia Dunmore and Judge Lillie Blackmon Sanders, thank you for investing in my life. I'm grateful!

Thank you to my coaches and sponsors, Dr. Christopher Ann Robinson-Easley, Dr. William (Marty) Martin, Candi Castelberry Singleton, and Fred T. Abbott, for believing and putting your creditability on the line for me.

To my spiritual imparters, Pastor Bruce and Lady Elaine Williams, Drs. Meredith and Marilyn Shackelford, Bishop Glen and Lady Kim Miller—thank you all for loving me and allowing me to vent and cry on your shoulders. I'm decreeing your latter will be greater than your past!

And finally, my creative teams—*Round Table Companies:* Corey, Katie, Erin, Kristin, Nadja, and Leeann; *Ace Fourggrafx:* Aaron; *Lee Graphix:* William; *220 Communications:* Glen; and *ND Enterprises:* Chanell Douglas. Thank you for helping make my dream a reality. I will never forget any of you. Many, many blessings to each of you!

Giving Flight to
Hopes and Dreams

WINGS helps homeless and abused women and children by offering integrated services that meet their needs for shelter, education, guidance, and support. WINGS residents, board of directors, and staff appreciate the kindness and consideration of all those who assist in our mission to end domestic violence and homelessness one family at a time. If you would like to make a donation you may mail this form or make a donation online. Thank you for traveling on this journey with us.

WINGS | P.O. Box 95615 | Palatine, IL 60095
www.wingsprogram.com/donate.htm

Name _____

Address _____

City/State/Zip _____

Phone (H) _____ (W) _____

☐ Amount enclosed $ _____

☐ Please charge my credit card
   for the following amount $ _____

   ☐ Visa   ☐ MasterCard   ☐ American Express

   Card number _____

   Exp. date _____ Security code _____

   Signature _____

☐ Please contact me regarding a major or planned gift or a gift to
   WINGS Endowment Fund.

    WINGS is a 501(c)(3) publicly supported organization.

When Trouble Finds You
Workbook

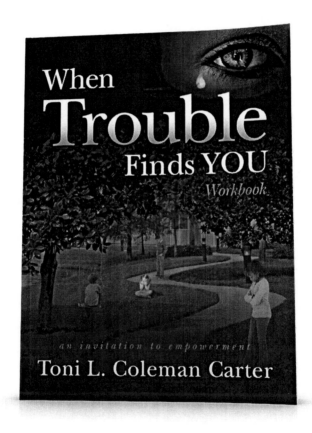

Available now from Amazon, Barnes & Noble,
Books-A-Million, and Powell's Books

CPSIA information can be obtained
at www.ICGtesting.com
Printed in the USA
EDOW021236310513
1753ED

9 781939 418043